martha stewart's
appetizers

martha stewart's
appetizers

200 recipes for dips, spreads, snacks, small plates,
and other delicious hors d'oeuvres, plus 30 cocktails

Clarkson Potter/
Publishers
New York

Contents

Foreword

In 1984 we published *Hors d'Oeuvres*, a lovely, useful book of recipes and entertaining ideas that enabled anyone to throw a great cocktail party with food that looked great, tasted delicious, and included many unique and unusual small bites. In 1999 we went a few steps further and published *Martha Stewart's Hors d'Oeuvres Handbook*, a much larger volume filled with new recipes, tips, building blocks, drinks, and party ideas that picked up where the first book had left off.

Now we're pleased to bring to you a new collection of recipes that reflects the new "casualness" we are all witnessing in home entertaining, a welcome relaxed approach to the serving of pre-dinner snacks, appetite enhancers, and small plates, accompanied by an interesting panoply of festive, flavorful cocktails that are easy to make and fun to serve.

This book, simply called *Appetizers*, is divided into five sections that are easy to understand and carefully designed to make the preparation of such Snacks, Starters, Small Plates, Stylish Bites, and Sips a joy. I encourage you to try all of the recipes as you maneuver your way through a year of celebrations, dinners, rites of passage, and other gatherings with friends and family. Revisit the cheese ball and make savory gougères, pureed vegetable dips that are addictive and healthy, four irresistible chicken wings, and many versions of the classic canapé, to name just a few of our favorites.

Enjoy, and let us know *your* favorites!

Martha Stewart

Golden Rules for Hosting a Party

1
keep the pantry stocked
Having basic and specialty items on hand means you can easily make appetizers for impromptu get-togethers and also get a jump-start when shopping for specific recipes.

2
make lists
Write down everything you will need: food, drinks, ice, plates and flatware, serving pieces, glasses, napkins, and any table decorations such as candles and flowers.

3
streamline the menu
Stick with one type of food—for example, an Asian-style menu of dumplings, summer rolls, and negimaki; or an all-American spread with hot artichoke dip, deviled eggs, and lobster rolls.

4
choose recipes wisely
Avoid trying too many new dishes; instead, include some old favorites in the mix, or test-drive any you'd like to serve *before* the event.

5
mix it up
Offer at least a few dishes that can be enjoyed by everyone, including options for those with food restrictions (e.g., vegan, nut-free, gluten-free).

6
think visually
Remember the presentation—are the starters served on platters or in bowls? is there a nice variety of colors and textures?—and choose appetizers that will please the eye as much as the palate.

7
front-load the work
Prepare as much food as you can ahead of time. Freeze-ahead dishes are especially helpful.

8
stick to your budget
Splurge on a few items if you like, and round out the menu with starters that are more affordable (seasoned popcorn or chips, for instance).

9
consider the drinks
Wine and beer are always appropriate, but a signature cocktail can really make a statement. Be sure to provide some nonalcoholic options.

10
relax and enjoy
A cool, calm, and collected host is always better company than someone who's rushing about. And remember: It's a party, not a competition.

Party Planning: Tips and Strategies

Any experienced host (or caterer) will tell you that a well-organized approach is the key to throwing a memorable party—for you and your guests.

Even if you are just having a couple of friends over for snacks and drinks, it pays to make a plan and stick to it. Just remember how much more relaxed you'll be if you follow the timeline as much as possible and don't end up with too many day-of tasks.

1 settle on a menu

Choosing the recipes can—and should—be one of the most enjoyable parts of throwing a party. Keep these considerations in mind:

- **Time of party:** The hour of the event will help determine what type of food, and how much, to offer. The earlier the party, the lighter the food can be. See How Much to Serve, *opposite.*

- **Guest count:** The fewer the guests, the fewer the items you'll need to serve. You can get by with two or three different starters at a party for six, whereas a celebratory event for 20 calls for a greater variety of hors d'oeuvres.

- **Tastes and textures:** When serving multiple dishes, think about how the different foods will taste together. Spicy food is fine, but you don't want to overload your guests with too much. Similarly, you'll want to offset rich foods with those that are fresh and light. And think about having a mix of crisp and crunchy, rich and creamy, tender and chewy—even hot and cold.

- **Recipe schedule:** Choose dishes that can be prepared, partially or entirely, in advance. They should also be easy to replenish. Think about your kitchen and what each recipe requires (so you don't end up using all the burners at once, or with more baking sheets than your oven can fit).

- **Personal preferences:** Odds are, if you're especially fond of something, your enthusiasm will spill over to your guests. Trends are fine to follow here and there, but don't overlook the appeal of all-time favorites like pigs in blankets, cheese balls, or a golden, bubbling baked dip.

2 establish a timeline

Chart the order in which you'll prepare certain recipes at the outset, when there's still time for tweaks. Consider adding more dishes that can be prepared at the same time (for example, one on the stove and one in the oven).

- For each recipe, start with when it will be served and work back to the present date, noting what can be made ahead, what needs to be done at the last minute, and everything in between.

- If there are make-ahead components, take note of storage information (including the containers) and how to finish the recipe. Pay special attention to frozen items: Some can go straight to the oven; others require thawing before cooking.

- Create a separate schedule for the day of the event, making sure to consider time spent on flowers, candles, or linens, chilling wine, as well as reheating anything made in advance.

- Once you've settled on the menu and gathered the necessary serving trays, platters, and bowls, put a note inside each one to mark what you plan to serve in it.

3 strategize your shopping

This cannot be empha-sized enough: Carefully read through the recipes as soon as you've finalized the menu. Give yourself enough time to buy what you need.

- Make a list of the ingredients for each recipe, and then cross off what you already have.

- Organize ingredients according to when they can be purchased—frozen goods and nonperishables well in advance, fresh produce and meats or fish a day or two ahead.

- Make a note of anything that needs to be special ordered (like cooked lobster meat or a baked ham).

- List any tools and equipment you will need to purchase (or borrow), and don't over-look serving pieces—skewers, spoons, spreaders, ramekins, and the like.

- Include beer, wine, and other spirits in your master plan. If making cocktails, note the ingredients and tools you will need (such as a muddler for mint juleps) as well as glasses and/or pitchers, punch bowls, or other serving vessels. And remember to include ice as well as any extra coolers.

HOW MUCH TO SERVE

Here are some tried-and-true suggestions for determining how many servings you will need, depending on the type and timing of your party.

- An afternoon get-together calls for simple snacks. Plan on one to two different offerings per guest.

- When hors d'oeuvres will be followed by a meal, they shouldn't be too filling; you could offer two or three differ-ent options, each yielding one to two servings per guest.

- If the party will extend through the dinner hour, offer more substantial dishes, such as dips, antipasto, or mezze spreads, and protein-packed dishes (sliders, shrimp, and chicken wings are all good options). Plan to offer three to five different items, each with at least three servings per guest.

WINNING FORMULA FOR AN HORS D'OEUVRE BUFFET

To feed ten people for two hours, you'll need about ten bite-size hors d'oeuvres per guest (for a total of 100 pieces). Start with one showstopper that can command the center of the table, and offer no more than three hot items (so you don't have to spend too much time in the kitchen). Remember to include options that address any dietary restrictions (vegetarian, nut-free, and gluten-free, for example). Use this formula to estimate the number of servings for a larger crowd.

TIP Cocktails fuel appetites, so plan for a bit more food than you think your guests might eat.

Party Planning 101: Serving Essentials

A lovely platter can turn a simple starter into something spectacular. This doesn't mean you have to shop for new pieces; you may already have some great household items that can be repurposed for entertaining. A slender vase could hold pastry straws, votive candleholders can be used for single-serving soups, and recycled tins are perfect for miniature biscuits.

A variety of shapes, sizes, and materials—wood, marble, stone, and ceramic, as examples—will add visual interest to a buffet, as long as they work in the same color palette. Start with this basic assortment, then tweak it accordingly.

Platters (1)
All food looks good on neutral white or cream-colored platters. Having multiple sizes and shapes—like the oval, square, and rectangular ones here—allows you to accommodate all types of appetizers.

Serving Spoons, Cocktail Forks, and Spreaders (2)
Use these for condiments and toppings, when guests will be serving themselves. Tiny cocktail forks are designed for scooping shellfish out and are the right size for dipping. Collect them in a variety of materials (horn, wood, and ceramic are all easy to find) as a nice alternative to using your everyday (or special-occasion) flatware.

Wooden Boards (3)
You probably have one or two of these workhorses in your kitchen already; cutting boards can also double as servers. Small boards are especially versatile; larger ones come in handy when you want to place extra items like condiments nearby. Lining the boards with parchment looks nice, and helps prevent staining.

Japanese Soup Spoons (4)
These ceramic spoons are ideal for holding dumplings and other bite-size items (one in each spoon).

Small Cups and Glasses (5)
Not just for drinking, petite vessels can be used for serving crudités or soups, too. You can also use them to corral cocktail skewers and toothpicks; set out a few empty ones for discards (and olive pits).

Pitchers (6)
These are a must for mixing—and serving—cocktails, like the ones shown on pages 240–41. Glass is best for drinks that are too colorful to hide. Don't forget a stirrer.

Trays (7)
Trays in various sizes make it easier to transport smaller dishes to and from the kitchen. Simple wooden ones go with everything, but you can find trays in all sorts of materials (silver, brass, melamine, glass, and lacquered engineered wood—to name a few) to suit any occasion.

Skewers and Toothpicks (8)
Toothpicks are handy for meatballs and other hors d'oeuvres that are too messy to eat with your fingers; cocktail skewers can serve the same purpose, besides being used for garnishing drinks. Plain wooden skewers make dipping bite-size pieces easy.

Small Bowls (9)
You can't have too many of these for serving dips and spreads, nuts and olives. Shallow ones make great vessels for dipping sauces.

Cocktail Plates (10)
Unless you are serving anything but the tiniest nibbles, you'll want to set out a stack of lightweight plates, since your guests will be juggling drinks and food—often while standing. Little plates are also handy if you want to arrange a few portions of starters around the room.

Paper Napkins (11)
White is always a good choice, but it's well worth picking up packs of patterned napkins whenever you come across something that you like. They keep forever, and you'll be glad to have a stash.

Marble and Stone Boards (12)
Because they are so good at retaining cold, marble and stone boards are excellent for serving cheese and fruit platters and other chilled or room temperature hors d'oeuvres (line with parchment to prevent stains).

Snacks

Consider these your new go-to crunchy, salty, tasty nibbles for casual get-togethers or for anytime friends are stopping by. Most can be assembled with items you're likely to have on hand, meaning you can delight in even the most impromptu occasions.

Simply the best one-ingredient, ultra-crisp "chip" you've ever tasted: Frico (shown on page 12), a specialty of the Friuli region of Italy, are just right for munching with a glass of Prosecco, of course, but also any other Italian wine, red or white.

A block of sharp feta makes an unexpected alternative to a wheel of creamy cheese and becomes wonderfully blistered and browned after only a few minutes under the broiler.

Frico
Makes 8

4 cups coarsely shredded
   Parmigiano-Reggiano cheese

1. Heat a large nonstick skillet over medium. For each frico, sprinkle ½ cup cheese evenly to cover bottom of pan. Cook until melted and golden, about 3 minutes.

2. Using a thin spatula, carefully lift cheese from skillet and drape over an inverted bowl (for a curved shape). Let cool until firm, then transfer to a wire rack to cool completely before serving.

NOTE For the most delicate, lacy texture, use cheese shredded on the large holes of a box grater—not finely grated cheese—and look for Parmigiano-Reggiano that was aged less than six months.

Broiled Feta
Serves 6 to 8

1 block feta cheese (8 ounces)
   Extra-virgin olive oil, for drizzling
   Fresh oregano, for serving
   Red-pepper flakes, for serving
   Pita breads, for serving

1. Heat broiler. Pat dry feta, and let stand at room temperature 30 minutes.

2. Transfer to a small baking dish, drizzle with the oil, and broil, turning once, until caramelized, 4 to 6 minutes. Top with the oregano, red-pepper flakes, and more oil. Serve with warmed pita breads, cut into wedges.

NOTE It's worth seeking out fresh varieties of feta (packed in water), which have a superior taste and texture to packaged cheese.

Stock your pantry with different nuts and spices, and you can make quick and easy snacks anytime. Best of all, seasoned nuts go hand in hand with practically any drink. They can also take on different flavors, like our six variations (clockwise, from the top left): Peppered Mixed Nuts with Lemon and Capers; Fried Herbed Almonds; Adobo Peanuts; Cayenne-Spiced Mixed Nuts; Sesame-Soy Cashews with Wasabi Peas and Nori; and Chinese Five-Spice Pecans. Each mix keeps well for a week or more.

Spiced Nuts

PEPPERED MIXED NUTS WITH LEMON AND FRIED CAPERS
makes 3 cups

1½ cups capers, preferably salt-packed

    Safflower oil, for frying

3 cups mixed roasted, unsalted nuts such as walnuts, blanched almonds, and hazelnuts

1 tablespoon finely grated lemon zest plus 1 tablespoon fresh lemon juice

1 teaspoon freshly ground pepper

1. Rinse and drain capers, transfer to a paper-towel-lined rimmed baking sheet, and gently pat dry with more paper towels. Let dry completely, about 1 hour.

2. Preheat oven to 300°F. In a saucepan, heat 2 inches oil until it registers 350°F on a deep-fry thermometer. In quarter-cup batches, carefully add capers and fry, stirring, until golden brown, about 3 minutes. Using a long-handled slotted spoon or mesh spider, transfer capers to a paper-towel-lined baking sheet to drain. Adjust heat as necessary to maintain oil temperature between batches. Reserve 2 tablespoons cooking oil; let cool.

3. In a bowl, toss nuts with reserved oil, lemon juice, and pepper. Spread in a single layer on a parchment-lined rimmed baking sheet. Bake, stirring occasionally, until golden brown, about 25 minutes. Let cool completely.

4. Sprinkle with lemon zest; toss with fried capers. Nuts can be stored in an airtight container at room temperature up to 1 week.

FRIED HERBED ALMONDS
makes 4 cups

1¼ cups plus 2 tablespoons extra-virgin olive oil

4 cups blanched almonds

¼ cup fresh thyme leaves

    Coarse salt and freshly ground pepper

Heat oil in a large skillet over medium. Add almonds and cook, stirring occasionally, until light golden and fragrant, 10 to 12 minutes. Stir in thyme. Remove from heat. Season generously with salt and pepper. Spread in a single layer on a parchment-lined rimmed baking sheet, and let cool completely. Nuts can be stored in an airtight container at room temperature up to 2 weeks.

NOTE You can also use Marcona almonds in this recipe; since they are often already fried in oil, simply heat them in a dry skillet before tossing with thyme and seasoning with salt and pepper.

Spiced Nuts

ADOBO PEANUTS
makes 3 cups

—

- ¼ cup sauce from 1 can (about 8 ounces) chipotle chiles in adobo sauce (reserve chiles and remaining sauce for another use)
- 2 tablespoons unsalted butter, melted
- ½ teaspoon coarse salt
- 3 cups roasted salted peanuts

1. Preheat oven to 350°F. Stir together adobo sauce, butter, and salt in a large bowl. Add peanuts and toss to coat.

2. Spread mixture in a single layer on a parchment-lined rimmed baking sheet. Bake, stirring occasionally, until sauce deepens in color and peanuts are toasted, about 20 minutes. Let cool completely. Nuts can be stored in an airtight container up to 2 weeks.

CAYENNE-SPICED MIXED NUTS
makes 5 cups

—

- 2 large egg whites
- ½ cup sugar
- 1 tablespoon cayenne pepper
- 2 teaspoons coarse salt
- 1 teaspoon dried chili powder
- 1 teaspoon ground cumin
- ½ teaspoon ground allspice
- 5 cups mixed nuts, such as peanuts, pecans, cashews, walnuts, and almonds

1. Preheat oven to 300°F. Whisk egg whites until foamy in a large bowl. Whisk in sugar, cayenne, salt, chili powder, cumin, and allspice, then add nuts and toss to coat.

2. Spread mixture in a single layer on a large parchment-lined rimmed baking sheet. Bake, stirring occasionally, 15 minutes. Reduce oven temperature to 250°F. Continue to bake nuts, stirring occasionally, until golden brown, about 10 minutes more. Let cool completely. Break up any nuts that stick together. Nuts can be stored in an airtight container at room temperature up to 2 weeks.

SESAME-SOY CASHEWS WITH WASABI PEAS AND NORI
makes 4 cups

___

  2 tablespoons low-sodium soy sauce

  1 tablespoon sugar

  ¾ teaspoon sake

  ½ teaspoon toasted sesame oil

  ½ teaspoon grated peeled fresh ginger

  ¼ teaspoon ground ginger

  2 cups roasted unsalted cashews

  ¼ cup sesame seeds

  ½ sheet toasted nori

  2 cups wasabi peas

1. Preheat oven to 250°F. In a large bowl, stir together soy sauce, sugar, sake, sesame oil, and fresh and ground ginger. Add cashews and sesame seeds, and toss to coat.

2. Spread mixture in a single layer on a parchment-lined rimmed baking sheet. Bake, stirring every 10 minutes, until glaze turns golden brown and is almost dry, about 40 minutes. Let cool completely.

3. Break nut mixture into clusters, and transfer to a bowl. Using kitchen scissors, cut nori into small pieces; add to bowl along with wasabi peas. Nuts can be stored in an airtight container at room temperature up to 1 week.

CHINESE FIVE-SPICE PECANS
makes 5 cups

___

  1 large egg white

  ⅓ cup packed dark-brown sugar

  ½ cup granulated sugar

  1 tablespoon low-sodium soy sauce

  1 teaspoon Chinese five-spice powder

  ½ teaspoon coarse salt

  5 cups pecans

1. Preheat oven to 250°F. Whisk egg white until foamy in a large bowl. Whisk in both sugars, soy sauce, five-spice powder, and salt. Add pecans and toss to coat.

2. Spread mixture in a single layer on a parchment-lined rimmed baking sheet. Bake, tossing occasionally, until golden brown, about 1 hour 10 minutes. Let cool completely. Nuts can be stored in an airtight container at room temperature up to 2 weeks.

You don't have to make party snacks entirely from scratch for them to be memorable. Start with the best-quality chips, then briefly warm them in the oven for a few minutes before sprinkling with the desired topping (shown opposite, from top to bottom): sea salt and black pepper; Old Bay seasoning; Japanese rice seasoning (see note below); malt-vinegar salt; and Parmesan and thyme.

Seasoned Potato Chips

—

serves 4

1 bag (10 to 13 ounces) potato chips
  Seasonings (recipes follow)

Preheat oven to 350°F. Spread potato chips in a single layer on a parchment-lined rimmed baking sheet and bake just until warm, about 3 minutes. Remove from oven, sprinkle with desired seasoning (add more to taste), and serve.

NOTE Japanese rice seasoning, called Furikake, is a popular condiment that's sprinkled over steamed rice for added flavor. It typically consists of nori or other seaweed, sesame seeds, bonito flakes, dried egg or vegetables, and salt and spices. You can find many varieties of the seasoning at Asian food markets and online; vegetarian options are also available.

SEA SALT AND BLACK PEPPER
Stir together 1¼ teaspoons flaky sea salt, such as Maldon, and ¾ freshly ground or cracked black pepper.

OLD BAY SEASONING
Use about 2½ teaspoons seasoning.

JAPANESE RICE SEASONING
See note, left. Use about 3 tablespoons seasoning.

MALT-VINEGAR SALT
makes ½ cup

—

Stir together ¼ cup plus 2 tablespoons coarse salt, 1 tablespoon cornstarch, and ¼ cup malt vinegar until a loose paste forms. Pour onto a rimmed baking sheet and spread into a thin layer. Let stand at room temperature (uncovered) 1 day. The paste will dry into a hard, cohesive sheet. Rake and mash sheet with a fork until it is the texture of wet sand. Malt-vinegar salt can be stored in an airtight container in a cool, dry place up to 3 months. Use about 2 tablespoons.

PARMESAN-THYME
Stir together ¼ cup plus 1 tablespoon finely grated Parmesan cheese and 2 tablespoons plus 1 teaspoon fresh thyme leaves.

We scaled down an easy drop biscuit recipe to make bite-size snacks easier for handling with drinks. We also added boosts of flavor from cheddar cheese and paprika in the dough, plus a bit more paprika that's sprinkled on the tops before baking. These can be made in less than an hour, and are best when still warm from the oven. In place of the cheddar and paprika, you can substitute Manchego and smoked pimentón.

Mini Cheese Biscuits

—

makes 74

2¼ cups all-purpose flour

1¼ teaspoons baking powder

¾ teaspoon baking soda

1 teaspoon coarse salt

2 teaspoons sugar

¾ teaspoon paprika, plus more for dusting

6 tablespoons cold unsalted butter, cut into pieces

1 cup finely grated cheddar cheese (6 ounces)

1½ cups heavy cream

1. Preheat oven to 375°F. Whisk together flour, baking powder, baking soda, salt, sugar, and paprika in a large bowl. Using a pastry blender or your fingers, cut butter into flour mixture until it resembles coarse meal, with a few larger clumps remaining. Stir in cheese with a fork. Add cream; stir until dough just comes together (it will be slightly sticky).

2. Scoop mounds of dough (about 2 teaspoons), 1½ inches apart, onto parchment-lined baking sheets. Lightly dust with paprika.

3. Bake until golden brown, rotating sheets halfway through, 15 to 20 minutes. Transfer biscuits (and parchment) onto wire racks to cool. Serve warm or at room temperature.

MAKE AHEAD Biscuits are best the same day but can be frozen in an airtight container up to 1 week; reheat in a 300°F oven, without thawing, for about 10 minutes.

Spiced Cream–Cheese Dips

Two dips are better (and just as easy) as one: Beat two 8-ounce bars of softened **cream cheese** with a mixer on medium-high until fluffy, 1 minute. Beat in ¾ teaspoon **coarse salt** and ½ cup chopped **scallions**. Divide between two bowls. Fold ½ cup **tomatillo salsa** (page 31 or store-bought) into one portion, and garnish with more scallions. Fold ½ cup **hot-pepper relish** into the other. Serve with **tortilla chips**.

Potatoes with Mascarpone and Roe

Set out all the components of this effortlessly elegant snack, and let guests serve themselves. Bring **fingerling potatoes** and water to cover by 2 inches to a boil in a saucepan; cook until just tender, about 10 minutes. Drain, cool, and halve lengthwise. To assemble, top one end with a dollop of **mascarpone cheese** and a spoonful of **salmon roe** (or other roe). Serve with your favorite bubbly.

Easy to prepare, fun to eat, and good for you, too—no wonder edamame have become so popular as a quick bite. Here, they are tossed while still warm with a spicy-sweet mixture of salt, red-pepper flakes, and sugar, but Japanese rice seasoning (see note, page 20) would also be good. Serve with chilled sake.

Edamame with Chile Salt

—

serves 4 to 6

½ teaspoon red-pepper flakes

1 tablespoon coarse salt

½ teaspoon sugar

1 pound frozen edamame in pods

1. Pulse red-pepper flakes in a spice grinder until finely ground. Transfer to a small bowl, and mix in salt and sugar.

2. Cook edamame in a large pot of boiling water until bright green and heated through, about 4 minutes. Drain and transfer to a large bowl. Toss with chile-salt mixture and serve warm.

These habit-forming nibbles just might become your new party favorite. You can adapt the basic formula to suit your own taste preferences, swapping out the cayenne and cumin for ground dried chiles, pimentón, or za'atar. Serve with a dry fino or oloroso sherry.

Roasted Spiced Chickpeas

—

serves 6 to 8

¼ cup extra-virgin olive oil

2 cans (15.5 ounces each) chickpeas, drained, rinsed, and patted dry

1 teaspoon cayenne pepper

1 tablespoon cumin seeds

    Coarse salt

1. Preheat oven to 450°F. Pour oil on a rimmed baking sheet, and heat in oven until hot, about 3 minutes.

2. Meanwhile, in a large bowl, toss to combine chickpeas, cayenne, and cumin. Season with salt.

3. Spread chickpea mixture in a single layer on hot baking sheet. Bake until chickpeas are crisp, stirring halfway through, 10 to 12 minutes. With a slotted spoon, transfer to paper towels to drain and cool slightly before serving.

There are countless recipes for the cereal-nut-pretzel-spice mix, but this one is especially tasty thanks to the addition of brown sugar, toffee bits, and browned butter infused with fresh thyme. You can switch up the type of nuts—try pecans or cashews in place of almonds—or use a mix of whatever types you have on hand.

Salty-Sweet Party Mix

serves 10

2 cups toasted cereal squares (such as whole-wheat and corn Chex)

¾ cup pretzel sticks

1 cup almonds

1 cup roasted unsalted peanuts

⅓ cup toffee bits

6 tablespoons unsalted butter

5 thyme sprigs

1 tablespoon packed dark-brown sugar

1 tablespoon mustard powder

2 teaspoons coarse salt

1. Preheat oven to 325°F. In a large bowl, combine cereal, pretzels, almonds, peanuts, and toffee.

2. Melt butter in a small saucepan over medium-high heat until golden brown, swirling occasionally, about 5 minutes. Remove from heat, and stir in thyme. (Butter will splatter.) Stir in brown sugar, mustard powder, and salt. Add to cereal mixture, and toss until evenly coated. Spread in an even layer on a rimmed baking sheet.

3. Bake, stirring halfway through, until nuts are toasted and toffee begins to melt, about 15 minutes. Let cool and discard thyme. Mix can be stored in an airtight container at room temperature up to 1 week.

Each of the following five salsas would be fine on its own, but offering two or three (or more) would be that much more fun (and not much more work). The salsa de árbol is the only one that requires any cooking; putting together the others is just a matter of chopping and stirring. Include the chile-pepper ribs and seeds for spicier salsa, and serve ice-cold beer and margaritas alongside to tame the heat.

Salsas

FRESH TOMATILLO SALSA
makes 2½ cups

Combine 1 pound quartered **tomatillos** (husked and washed), ⅓ cup chopped **white onion**, 1 chopped **jalapeño chile** (ribs and seeds removed if less heat is desired), ½ cup lightly packed **fresh cilantro** leaves and stems, and 3 tablespoons fresh **lime** juice in a food processor. Pulse until finely chopped; season with **coarse salt** and serve.

PICO DE GALLO
makes 1¾ cups

Combine 1 diced **tomato** (1 cup), ½ cup diced **white onion**, 2 diced small **serrano chiles** (ribs and seeds removed if less heat is desired), and 2 tablespoons chopped **fresh cilantro** leaves and stems in a bowl. Season with **coarse salt** and serve.

PINEAPPLE AND BLACK BEAN SALSA
makes 4 cups

Combine 1 can (15.5 ounces) **black beans**, drained and rinsed, 1½ cups chopped **pineapple**, 1 minced **jalapeño chile** (ribs and seeds removed if less heat is desired), 3 tablespoons finely chopped **red onion**, ¼ cup chopped **fresh cilantro** leaves and stems, and 1 tablespoon fresh **lime** juice in a bowl. Season with **coarse salt**. Salsa can be refrigerated, covered, up to 3 days.

CORN AND TOMATO RELISH
makes 2 cups

Combine 1 cup fresh **corn kernels** (from 2 ears corn), 1 diced **tomato** (1 cup), 1 thinly sliced **scallion**, 2 tablespoons chopped **fresh cilantro** leaves and stems, and 1 tablespoon fresh **lime** juice in a large bowl. Season with **coarse salt** and freshly ground **pepper**. Salsa can be refrigerated, covered, up to 1 day.

SALSA DE ÁRBOL
makes 2 cups

Heat a large cast-iron skillet over medium-high. Add 1 pound **tomatillos** (husked and washed); cook, turning occasionally, until blistered in spots and beginning to soften, 10 to 12 minutes. Transfer to a bowl, cover with plastic wrap, and let steam 15 minutes.

Meanwhile, cook 6 **garlic** cloves in skillet over medium, turning occasionally, until blistered and fragrant, 1 to 2 minutes. Transfer to a blender.

Combine 8 **dried chiles de árbol** and 4 **dried pasilla or New Mexico chiles** (all stemmed) in skillet; cook, turning frequently, just until toasted and soft, 30 to 60 seconds. Transfer to blender along with tomatillos and accumulated juices and 2 tablespoons **water**. Puree until smooth, about 10 seconds. Season with **coarse salt**. Salsa can be refrigerated, covered, up to 1 week; bring to room temperature before serving.

Serve crisp radishes with soft, spreadable butter and coarse salt for a snack that's French through and through. Here, a mixture of fresh chives and parsley flavors the butter; other options include dill, tarragon, thyme, or oregano.

Radishes with Mixed-Herb Butter and Sea Salt

—

serves 4

½ cup (1 stick) unsalted butter, room temperature

¼ cup finely chopped mixed fresh herbs, such as chives and flat-leaf parsley

2 bunches radishes, scrubbed, large ones halved, leaves intact, if desired

Flaky sea salt (such as Maldon) or coarse salt, for serving

Mix together butter and herbs in a small bowl. Serve immediately, or refrigerate, covered, up to 1 week; bring to room temperature before serving, with radishes and salt (for sprinkling).

Fast and fresh: With dried chili powder, salt, and lime, you can create a speedy (and healthy) snack from sliced pineapple, mango, and papaya—or any one of these will do. The tropical flavors call for beer or a rum-based cocktail, like the daiquiris on page 241.

Papaya, Mango, and Pineapple with Spiced Salt

—

serves 4

2 teaspoons ancho chili powder

1 tablespoon coarse salt

1 pineapple, peeled, cut into spears

1 mango, peeled, pitted, and cut into spears

1 papaya, peeled, cut into spears

Lime wedges, for serving

Mix together chili powder and salt in a small bowl. Arrange fruit on a platter, then sprinkle with chili-salt and a squeeze of lime. Serve immediately, with more lime wedges.

A big bowl of seasoned popcorn goes a long way, and it doesn't take long to replenish it as needed. There's a secret to getting every last kernel to pop (let stand 30 seconds), but this is among the easiest of snacks to make, in a variety of flavors (shown opposite, from top to bottom): sea salt-pepper; chili-lime; sesame-pepper; Pecorino-rosemary; smoked paprika; and spicy-sweet.

Seasoned Popcorn

—

serves 6

¼ cup safflower oil

½ cup popcorn kernels

Seasonings (recipes follow)

Heat oil and a few popcorn kernels in a large, heavy-bottomed pot over high heat. When kernels pop, add remaining kernels and cover. Remove from heat; let stand 30 seconds. Return to heat and cook, shaking pot frequently, until popping stops, 1 to 2 minutes. Toss with desired seasonings (adding more to taste), transfer to a bowl, and serve immediately.

SEA SALT-PEPPER

Stir together 1 tablespoon flaky sea salt, such as Maldon, and ¾ teaspoon freshly ground or cracked black pepper.

CHILI-LIME

Combine 1¼ teaspoons chili powder, 1¼ teaspoons cumin, ½ teaspoon coarse salt, and 1 tablespoon finely grated lime zest in a large bowl. Add hot popcorn, and squeeze juice from 1 large lime wedge into bowl. Toss until evenly coated.

SESAME-PEPPER

Grind 2 tablespoons black sesame seeds, lightly toasted, 1 teaspoon coarse salt, and ½ teaspoon freshly ground pepper in a spice grinder until seeds are coarsely ground. Toss hot popcorn with 2 tablespoons melted unsalted butter until evenly coated, then toss with sesame mixture.

PECORINO-ROSEMARY

Stir together 3 tablespoons finely grated Pecorino Romano cheese and 3 teaspoons chopped fresh rosemary.

SMOKED PAPRIKA

Season with coarse salt to taste, then add 1½ teaspoons smoked paprika, also called pimentón.

SPICY-SWEET

Combine 1½ teaspoons granulated brown sugar (or light-brown sugar, sifted), ¾ teaspoon coarse salt, 1 teaspoon garam masala, and ⅛ teaspoon cayenne pepper in a small bowl. Toss hot popcorn with 2 tablespoons melted unsalted butter until evenly coated, then toss with brown-sugar mixture.

Shishito Peppers with Bonito Flakes

Try this popular tapas bar snack, with a Japanese twist: Heat a skillet over medium-high; add **shishito** (or Padrón) **peppers** and drizzle with **extra-virgin olive oil**; cook, tossing, until blistered in spots, about 5 minutes. Remove from heat. Sprinkle with finely grated **lime** zest, lime juice, **flaky sea salt**, and **bonito flakes.** Serve immediately, with sake—or Spanish cava.

Watermelon Wedges with Feta and Mint

The contrast of cool, sweet melon and salty, creamy cheese is one reason to make this summer appetizer; the fact that it's so easy is another. Cut a small seedless **watermelon** into 1-inch-thick wedges. Arrange on a platter, and top with finely crumbled **feta cheese** and small **fresh mint** leaves; then sprinkle with freshly ground **pepper** and serve.

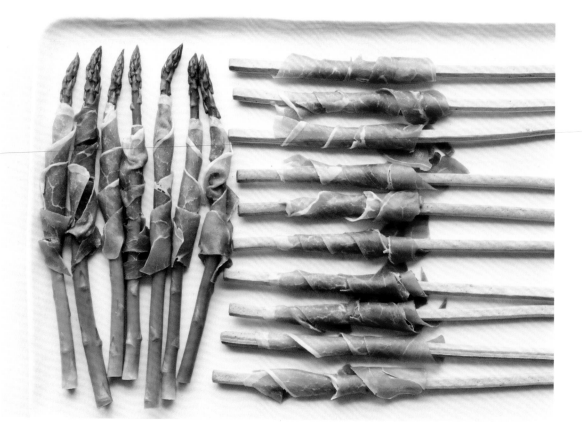

You can wrap paper-thin slices of prosciutto around more than just melon wedges. Here, crunchy breadsticks and crisp-yet-tender steamed asparagus spears are two fun, super-slim options.

Prosciutto-Wrapped Asparagus and Breadsticks

—

serves 4

16 thin stalks asparagus, tough ends trimmed

8 ounces thinly sliced prosciutto

16 grissini or other thin breadsticks

1. Place asparagus spears in a steamer basket set in a saucepan with an inch of water. Bring water to a boil, then reduce to a simmer. Cover and steam asparagus until bright green and just tender, about 2 minutes. Transfer to an ice-water bath, and let cool completely. Drain and pat dry.

2. Wrap 1 slice prosciutto around each asparagus spear and grissini, leaving about 1 inch of tips exposed, and serve.

Dried figs become a savory-sweet starter when tossed with extra-virgin olive oil, honey, and salt, and roasted until caramelized. A mix of Turkish and Black Mission figs—and a cluster of red grapes—makes a pretty platter to serve with drinks. Try a fruity Italian red wine such as Barbera or Nebbiolo.

Honey-Roasted Salted Figs

—

serves 6

¼ cup extra-virgin olive oil, plus more for baking sheet

¼ cup clover honey

10 ounces dried Turkish figs

10 ounces dried Black Mission figs

Coarse salt

Grapes, such as red champagne, for serving

1. Preheat oven to 400°F. In a large bowl, whisk together oil and honey. Add figs; toss to coat. Arrange in a single layer on a lightly oiled rimmed baking sheet. Sprinkle with salt.

2. Roast until fragrant and caramelized, 12 to 15 minutes. Immediately loosen figs from sheet with a metal spatula. Let figs cool slightly, loosening again after 5 minutes. Transfer to a platter; serve warm with grapes.

Sure, you can find plenty of options when it comes to buying olives from a specialty-foods store (and even the supermarket), but it's a fast, simple process to dress them up yourself, and with fresher-tasting results. Choose olives in different shapes and colors for a more interesting presentation, like the Cerignola, Castelvetrano, Kalamata, and Niçoise shown here.

Warmed Olives

—

serves 4 to 6

2 cups assorted olives, rinsed and drained

¾ cup extra-virgin olive oil

2 to 3 thin strips orange or lemon zest

2 small sprigs rosemary or thyme

Red-pepper flakes

Combine olives, oil, orange zest, and rosemary in a skillet. Season with red-pepper flakes. Bring to a simmer, and cook, stirring occasionally, until warmed through, about 5 minutes. With a slotted spoon, transfer olives and seasonings to a bowl; reserve oil for another use (see tip, right). Serve warm.

TIP Reserve the flavorful oil used to cook the olives for making vinaigrettes or drizzling over roasted vegetables, fish, or chicken.

Lip-smacking nibbles, Italian style: Stuff large olives with blue cheese, coat them with egg and breadcrumbs, then fry to a crisp, golden crust. Salty flavors like this call for Lambrusco, an Italian bubbly that's a more robust alternative to prosecco or other sparkling white wines.

Fried Stuffed Olives

—

makes 24

24 large pitted green olives, such as Manzanilla or Sicilian

2 ounces blue cheese, such as gorgonzola or roquefort

3 tablespoons all-purpose flour

1 large egg, lightly beaten

½ cup plain dried bread-crumbs (see page 242)

2 cups safflower oil

1. Soak olives in cold water for 15 minutes. Drain and pat dry. Stuff each with cheese.

2. Put flour, egg, and breadcrumbs in three separate bowls. Dredge olives in flour, dip in egg, then dredge in breadcrumbs.

3. Heat oil in a saucepan over medium until hot but not smoking. Working in batches, fry olives until golden brown, about 1½ minutes. Use a slotted spoon to transfer to a paper-towel-lined plate to drain. Serve warm.

MAKE AHEAD Breaded olives can be refrigerated on a parchment-lined rimmed baking sheet until ready to fry, up to 4 hours.

Olive lovers—and there are legions—will look for any opportunity to use the briny fruits. These three spreads are seasoned with herbs, lemon, and other fresh flavors. Serve them with crostini or toasted pita, or as part of a mezze spread (see pages 140 to 143).

Olive Spreads

BLACK-OLIVE AND PINE-NUT RELISH
makes 1½ cups

▬

Combine ½ cup chopped pitted **oil-cured black olives**, 2 tablespoons **pine nuts**, ½ minced small **garlic clove**, 2 tablespoons chopped **fresh flat-leaf parsley** leaves, and ½ teaspoon chopped **fresh rosemary**; transfer to a bowl. Add 6 **cherry tomatoes**, quartered, 1 tablespoon finely grated **lemon** zest, and 1 tablespoon plus 1½ teaspoons **extra-virgin olive oil**; mix to combine. Relish can be refrigerated, covered, up to 1 day; bring to room temperature before serving.

OLIVE-CAPER TAPENADE
makes 1½ cups

▬

In a food processor, pulse 2 cups pitted **brine-cured black olives**, 1 cup **fresh flat-leaf parsley** leaves, 2 tablespoons rinsed and drained **capers**, finely grated zest and juice of 1 **lemon**, and 2 rinsed and patted dry **anchovy fillets** until finely chopped. With the motor running, add 2 tablespoons **extra-virgin olive oil**; process just until a paste forms. Transfer to a bowl. Tapenade can be refrigerated, covered, up to 1 week; bring to room temperature before serving.

GREEN-OLIVE AND PARSLEY RELISH
makes 1½ cups

▬

With a sharp knife, slice away peel and pith of 1 **lemon**. Cut flesh into segments; coarsely chop and transfer to a bowl. Add 1 cup coarsely chopped pitted **green olives**, 1 tablespoon minced **red onion**, 1 finely chopped **celery** stalk, ¼ teaspoon **sugar**, 3 tablespoons **extra-virgin olive oil**, and 3 tablespoons **fresh flat-leaf parsley** leaves. Season with **coarse salt** and freshly ground **pepper** and stir to combine. Relish can be refrigerated, covered, up to 1 day; bring to room temperature, and stir in parsley just before serving.

Starters

The cocktail hour is an opportunity to engage dinner guests and make them feel warm, welcome, and eager for a night of good food and conversation. But don't fill them up—offer little bites of pure enjoyment to spark their appetites.

Delicate, airy, and delectable, gougères (French cheese puffs) are practically foolproof. They also freeze well before baking (keep a few batches tucked away for impromptu parties). Pâte à choux—or "cabbage paste," since it resembles little cabbages after baking—is quickly mixed on the stovetop, then the eggs are beaten in, a two-step process that results in the very best texture. A pastry bag and a large plain tip make fast work of piping the puffs.

Gougères

CLASSIC GOUGÈRES
makes about 48

▬

- ½ cup (1 stick) unsalted butter
- 1 teaspoon salt
- 1 cup all-purpose flour
- 5 to 6 large eggs
- ½ cup finely grated Gruyère cheese

1. Preheat oven to 375°F. In a saucepan, bring 1 cup water, the butter, and salt to a boil. Cook, stirring, until butter is melted. Remove from heat; add flour. Stir with a wooden spoon until combined. Stir constantly over medium heat until dough pulls away from sides of pan and leaves a film on bottom of pan, 2 to 4 minutes.

2. Transfer to a mixing bowl. Beat on medium speed until mixture cools slightly, about 1 minute. Beat in 4 eggs, incorporating each one before adding the next. Dough should be shiny and a string should form when you touch the surface and then lift it with your finger. If no string forms, lightly beat another egg; add a little at a time. (If a string still doesn't form, add water, 1 teaspoon at a time.) Mix in cheese.

3. Transfer dough to a pastry bag fitted with a plain ½-inch tip (Ateco #804). Pipe 1½-inch rounds, 2 inches apart, onto parchment-lined baking sheets. Smooth peaks with your fingertip.

4. In a bowl, whisk remaining egg and 1 tablespoon water; brush over mounds. Bake 20 to 25 minutes. Prop open oven door with a wooden spoon; bake until gougères are puffed and golden, 3 to 5 minutes more. Transfer sheets to wire racks to cool. Serve warm.

MIXED HERB
Add 2 tablespoons finely chopped mixed **fresh herbs,** such as dill, thyme, tarragon, and oregano, to dough along with the cheese at the end of step 2.

LEMON-PARSLEY
Add 2 tablespoons finely chopped **fresh flat-leaf parsley** and finely grated zest of 1 **lemon** (1 tablespoon) to dough along with the cheese at the end of step 2.

BACON-CHEDDAR
Substitute Gruyère with an equal amount of finely grated **cheddar cheese** and add 2 tablespoons finely chopped **cooked bacon** (from 2 slices) to dough along with the cheese at the end of step 2.

MANCHEGO-CUMIN
Substitute Gruyère with an equal amount of finely grated **Manchego cheese** and add ½ teaspoon crushed toasted **cumin seeds** (see page 242) to dough along with the cheese at the end of step 2.

MAKE AHEAD Gougères can be prepared through step 3 and frozen on baking sheets until firm; transfer to resealable plastic bags, and freeze up to 3 weeks. Bake straight from the freezer for a few minutes more than directed. Baked gougères can also be frozen in an airtight container up to 1 month; reheat them (without thawing) in a 350°F oven until warmed through, about 10 minutes, before serving.

Cheese balls have a lot going for them: They're always creamy and delicious and usually coated in something fun and flavorful, like crunchy pecans or chopped bacon. More than anything, they're simple to make (even a day ahead), relying on only a handful of ingredients. We flavored our classic version with mango chutney, swirled ruby port into another, and spiked a blue-cheese ball with hot-pepper sauce. Make just one flavor or all three, and serve with your favorite crackers, toasts, chips, or crudité.

Cheese Balls

CLASSIC CHEESE BALL
serves 10

Grate 8 ounces **cheddar cheese** to yield 2 cups, and let come to room temperature along with 1 bar (8 ounces) **cream cheese** and 4 tablespoons **unsalted butter**.

With an electric mixer on medium speed, beat cheddar, cream cheese, butter, 1 tablespoon **milk**, and 1 tablespoon **mango chutney** until combined. Transfer to a bowl, cover, and refrigerate until firm, at least 8 hours.

Shape cheese mixture into a ball. Place 1 cup chopped toasted **pecans** (see page 242) on a plate. Roll cheese ball in nuts to coat. Serve at room temperature.

AGED-CHEDDAR AND PORT
serves 10

Bring ¼ cup **ruby port** to a simmer over low heat in a small saucepan. Cook until reduced by about half, about 30 minutes. Let cool completely.

Grate 8 ounces aged **cheddar cheese** to yield 2 cups, and let come to room temperature along with 1 bar (8 ounces) **cream cheese**.

With an electric mixer on medium speed, beat cheddar with three-quarters bar cream cheese until smooth. In another bowl, beat remaining one-quarter bar cream cheese with reduced port. Gently stir port mixture into cheddar mixture until just swirled together. Cover; refrigerate until firm, at least 8 hours.

Shape cheese mixture into a ball. Place 1 cup chopped **dried cranberries** on a plate. Roll cheese ball in fruit to coat. Serve at room temperature.

BLUE CHEESE, BACON, AND SCALLION
serves 10

Crumble 8 ounces **Roquefort cheese** to yield 2 cups, and let come to room temperature along with 1 bar (8 ounces) **cream cheese**.

With an electric mixer on medium speed, beat Roquefort, cream cheese, 2 teaspoons fresh **lemon** juice, a few dashes of **hot sauce** (such as Tabasco), and ¼ teaspoon **coarse salt** until combined. Transfer to a bowl, cover, and refrigerate until firm, at least 8 hours.

Cook 6 slices **bacon** in a large skillet over medium heat until golden and most of fat is rendered, 6 to 8 minutes. Transfer to paper towels to drain, then finely chop and combine with 6 finely chopped **scallions** on a plate.

Shape cheese mixture into a ball. Roll cheese ball in bacon-scallion mixture to coat. Serve at room temperature.

MAKE AHEAD Cheese balls can be refrigerated up to 3 days (without the coatings). You can also coat them the same day and keep in the refrigerator; let stand at room temperature for 1 hour before serving.

No-cook toppings are the perfect dinner-party starter, when your oven and stovetop might already be in use. Start by making crostini (up to a day ahead), then top with ricotta followed by simple ingredients, depending on the season: watercress in the spring; cherry tomatoes and basil in the summer; sliced pear, honey, and walnuts in the fall; grated lemon zest and black pepper or chutney in the winter—or all year long.

Ricotta Crostini

—

makes about 24

1 baguette, thinly sliced
  Extra-virgin olive oil
2½ cups ricotta cheese
  Coarse salt
  Toppings (recipes follow)

1. Preheat oven to 350°F. Arrange bread slices in a single layer on a rimmed baking sheet. Brush both sides with oil, and bake until lightly toasted and crisp, 8 to 10 minutes. Transfer to a wire rack to cool completely.

2. To serve, dollop ricotta onto each crostini, season with coarse salt, and top as desired.

MAKE AHEAD Crostini can be stored in an airtight container up to 1 day at room temperature before topping and serving.

LEMON AND PEPPER
Drizzle crostini with **extra-virgin olive oil**, then sprinkle with finely grated **lemon** zest, freshly ground **pepper**, and **flaky sea salt** (such as Maldon).

WATERCRESS
Top each toast with a sprig of **watercress**, drizzle with **extra-virgin olive oil**, and sprinkle with **coarse salt**.

CHUTNEY
Dollop each toast with **mango chutney** (or any flavor of chutney). Sprinkle with freshly ground **pepper**.

TOMATO AND BASIL
Top each toast with 3 to 4 **cherry- or grape-tomato** halves and a sprig of **basil**. Drizzle with **extra-virgin olive oil** and sprinkle with **flaky sea salt** (such as Maldon).

PEAR AND PECANS
Top each toast with a few slices of ripe **pear**, such as Bartlett or Anjou, a few chopped toasted **pecans** (see page 242), and a drizzle of **honey**.

Is it a dressing or a dip? Who cares? Green goddess dressing, the beloved California creation, doubles as a dip for a summertime crudité platter. The creamy concoction is studded with chopped fresh herbs and scallions, and it pairs particularly well with the season's bounty—here, baby carrots and yellow squash, tender peas and beans, and little tomatoes—but let the greenmarket (or your own garden) be your guide.

Summer Crudités with Green Goddess Dip

—

serves 6 to 8

1 cup sour cream

⅔ cup mayonnaise

2 anchovy fillets, preferably salt packed, rinsed

1½ cups fresh flat-leaf parsley leaves

½ cup fresh basil leaves

4 scallions, trimmed and chopped, dark-green tops reserved

Coarse salt and freshly ground pepper

¼ cup chopped fresh tarragon leaves

Assorted crudités, such as cherry tomatoes, baby carrots, and blanched snap peas, snow peas, wax beans, and baby squash (see note), for serving

1. In a food processor, puree sour cream, mayonnaise, anchovies, parsley, basil, and chopped scallions until smooth. Season with salt and pepper. Transfer to a bowl. Refrigerate, covered, up to 1 day.

2. Finely chop reserved dark-green scallion tops and stir into dip, along with tarragon. Season with salt and pepper. Serve with crudités.

NOTE Working in separate batches, blanch snow and snap peas, wax beans, and squash in a pot of salted boiling water until just tender, about 1 minute for peas and beans, 2 minutes for squash; use a slotted spoon to transfer vegetables to an ice-water bath, and let cool completely before removing and patting dry. Halve squash lengthwise before serving.

Creamy whites and the palest shades of green compose this cool wintry crudité assortment. The delectable dip has both buttermilk and crème fraîche, and deserves to be put into your regular appetizer rotation year-round. It is delicious with any seasonal vegetables—and potato chips, of course.

Winter Crudités with Buttermilk Dip

—

serves 6 to 8

1 cup buttermilk

1 cup crème fraîche or sour cream

½ cup coarsely chopped fresh dill

¼ teaspoon finely grated lemon zest

1 tablespoon plus 1½ teaspoons fresh lemon juice

Pinch of cayenne pepper

Coarse salt and freshly ground black pepper

Assorted crudités, such as celery stalks, hearts of romaine, icicle radishes, cucumber spears, and blanched cauliflower florets and white asparagus (see note), for serving

1. Combine buttermilk, crème fraîche, dill, lemon zest and juice, and cayenne in a bowl. Season with salt and black pepper. Refrigerate, covered, up to 1 day; stir until smooth before serving.

2. Arrange crudités in glasses (or on a platter), and serve with dip.

NOTE White asparagus is typically tougher than the green variety, so it's a good idea to peel the stalks, beginning about 2 inches below tips and working toward the opposite ends, before blanching in a pot of salted boiling water until just tender, about 1 minute. Use tongs to transfer to an ice-water bath, and let cool completely before removing and patting dry. Blanch cauliflower in same pot, about 3 minutes; remove with a slotted spoon, pat dry, and let cool (do not transfer to ice bath).

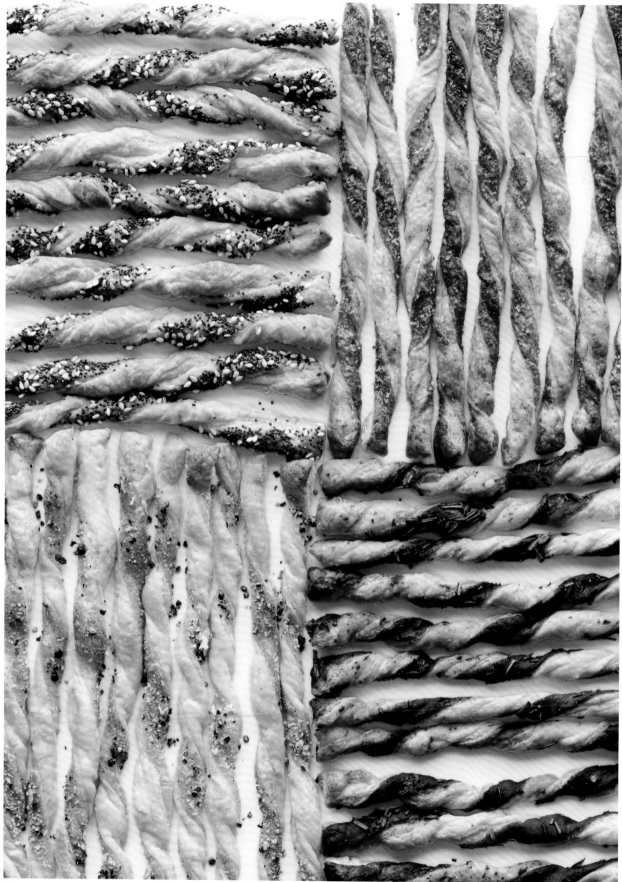

These twisty hors d'oeuvres just keep on giving: Everyone loves them, they are easy to eat out of hand, and they pair well with practically any drink. For more recipes made with store-bought puff pastry (a great shortcut), see the Provençal Onion Tart (page 80) and Puff Pastry Tarts (page 151).

Puff Pastry Cheese Straws

—

makes about 30

1 cup finely grated Parmigiano-Reggiano cheese (about 4 ounces)

½ teaspoon cayenne pepper

2 sheets frozen puff pastry, preferably all-butter, thawed

   All-purpose flour, for dusting

2 large eggs, lightly beaten

1. Preheat oven to 425°F. Combine cheese and cayenne in a bowl.

2. Lay each puff pastry sheet flat on a lightly floured work surface. Roll out to 11-by-16-inch rectangles. Dividing evenly, brush with some of beaten eggs and sprinkle with cheese mixture. Using a pastry cutter or sharp paring knife, trim long ends to make even, and cut each rectangle crosswise into fifteen ½-inch-wide strips.

3. Working with one at a time, twist strips into a spiral, and transfer to parchment-lined baking sheets, 1 inch apart. Using your thumb, press the ends of the strips onto the parchment to prevent unraveling during baking. Chill until firm, at least 30 minutes.

4. Bake until pastry is golden, rotating sheets halfway through, 10 to 15 minutes. Transfer sheets to wire racks, and let puff pastry straws cool completely before serving or storing.

SESAME-POPPY
Combine 2 tablespoons each **sesame seeds** and **poppy seeds** with ¼ teaspoon **coarse salt** in a bowl. Sprinkle on pastry strips instead of cheese-cayenne mixture.

TOMATO-ROSEMARY
Omit egg wash and cheese-cayenne mixture. Combine 3 tablespoons **tomato paste** and 1 tablespoon **extra-virgin olive oil** in a bowl. Brush evenly on pastry strips, then sprinkle with 1 tablespoon chopped **fresh rosemary**.

PECORINO-BLACK PEPPER
Substitute Parmigiano-Reggiano with an equal amount of **Pecorino Romano cheese**, and **cayenne pepper** with freshly ground **black pepper**. Sprinkle this mixture on pastry strips.

MAKE AHEAD Straws can be prepared through step 3 up to 1 month ahead; cover tightly with plastic wrap, and freeze until firm, about 1 hour. Then transfer to resealable plastic bags, and freeze until ready to bake (without thawing). After baking, straws will keep up to 1 day in an airtight container at room temperature.

ABOUT PUFF PASTRY Whenever possible, use all-butter varieties, such as Trader Joe's or Dufour, for the best flavor and texture. For even thawing, let puff pastry sit in the refrigerator overnight, rather than on the counter, which can cause the pastry to become sticky and difficult to work with.

These crisp-on-the-outside rice balls are deeply cheesy—in the best possible way. You can spread the preparation over a couple of days: Cook the risotto through step 2 on one day, let cool, and refrigerate. Form into balls, stuff with cheese, and chill on the baking sheet the next day. Then fry just before serving, in all their ooey-gooey glory.

Arancini
—

makes about 30

4 tablespoons unsalted butter

2 shallots, finely diced (½ cup)

1 cup arborio rice

½ cup dry white wine

4 cups low-sodium chicken broth, warmed

¼ cup finely grated Parmigiano-Reggiano cheese

2 tablespoons chopped fresh sage, plus small leaves for serving

Coarse salt and freshly ground pepper

6 ounces Taleggio cheese, rind removed, cut into ½-inch cubes

½ cup all-purpose flour

2 large eggs

2 cups panko

Safflower oil, for frying

Flaky sea salt (such as Maldon), for serving

TIP You can use a small pot or a deep straight-sided skillet when deep frying; those made of cast iron retain heat better than others, which is important when cooking in batches (since the oil temperature should remain steady). A couple other rules to follow: Don't fill the pan more than halfway with oil, to avoid spatters; and don't overcrowd the pan, which will prevent each ball from forming a crisp crust.

1. Heat 2 tablespoons butter in a medium saucepan over medium. Add shallots; cook, stirring occasionally, until tender, about 4 minutes. Add rice and cook, stirring, until toasted, about 1 minute. Add wine and cook, stirring, until absorbed.

2. Gradually add broth, 1 cup at a time, stirring until almost absorbed before adding more broth, until rice is just tender, 20 to 25 minutes. (You may not need all the broth.) Remove from heat, and stir in remaining 2 tablespoons butter and the parmesan. Add sage; season with salt and pepper. Spread risotto in a 9-by-13-inch baking dish. Let cool completely. (If making ahead, cover and refrigerate up to 1 day.)

3. Form risotto into 1½-inch balls. Insert a cube of Taleggio in the center of each. Place flour, eggs, and panko in three shallow dishes; lightly beat eggs. Dredge each ball with flour, shaking off excess, dip in eggs, then coat in panko and transfer to a parchment-lined baking sheet.

4. Heat 2 inches oil in a heavy-bottomed pot over medium-high until 360°F on a deep-fry thermometer. Working in batches, fry balls until golden brown, turning once, about 3 minutes per batch. Use a slotted spoon to transfer to paper towels to drain. Sprinkle with sea salt. Return oil to 360°F between batches.

5. Fry small sage leaves in oil until crisp and bright green, about 30 seconds. Transfer to paper towels to drain. Top risotto balls with fried sage and serve immediately.

NOTE To keep them warm while you finish frying batches, place arancini on a parchment-lined baking sheet in a 225°F oven.

It may look like an ordinary ball of fresh mozzarella, but burrata—"buttery" in Italian—boasts a wonderfully rich interior of mozzarella blended with cream. It's the starting point for a dish that's luscious and almost too easy to be true, especially if you opt to use pickled hot cherries from a jar instead of making your own (though that takes mere minutes to do, and can be finished well in advance).

Burrata with Hot Pickled Peppers

—

serves 8

1 pound hot cherry peppers, washed well and dried

3 garlic cloves, halved

2 dried bay leaves

½ teaspoon whole black peppercorns

2 cups white-wine vinegar (at least 5 percent acidity)

2 tablespoons sugar

¾ teaspoon coarse salt

2 balls (8 ounces each) burrata cheese, room temperature

   Extra-virgin olive oil, for drizzling

   Baguette or other rustic bread, for serving

1. Trim cherry pepper stems. Combine peppers, garlic, bay leaves, and peppercorns in a heatproof nonreactive container.

2. Bring vinegar, ¾ cup water, the sugar, and salt to a simmer in a medium saucepan over medium heat. Cook, stirring, until sugar dissolves. Pour hot pickling liquid over peppers. Let cool completely, then refrigerate in an airtight container at least 1 hour and up to 1 month.

3. Place burrata in a dish, and break it open with a spoon. Drizzle with oil. Top with a few pickled peppers (break some in half, if desired) and serve with bread.

NOTE Serve extra pickled peppers as part of an antipasto spread (either on their own or in place of jarred peppers for the cheese-stuffed version on page 119) or relish tray. Or slice and layer in frittatas or on crostini. They also make great garnishes for cocktails.

The sauce that's usually served for shrimp cocktail is nothing more than equal parts ketchup and prepared horseradish. We've updated it with three new options, each also made with just two ingredients: lemon and dill; Sriracha and mayonnaise; and miso and butter. Pile the shrimp on an ice-filled platter and they're ready to serve.

Shrimp Cocktail with Three Sauces

—

serves 8

1 lemon, halved

2 dried bay leaves

Coarse salt

2 pounds shell-on large shrimp (16 to 20 count)

Two-Ingredient Sauces (recipes follow), for serving

Prepare a large ice-water bath. Bring a large pot of water to a boil; add lemon, bay leaves, and a generous amount of salt. Reduce heat, add shrimp, and simmer until bright pink and opaque, 3 to 4 minutes. Drain and transfer shrimp to the ice bath to cool completely, then drain again. Serve over ice, with sauces alongside.

MAKE AHEAD Once cool, boiled shrimp can be refrigerated, covered, up to 1 day.

ABOUT SHRIMP Most shrimp is flash-frozen before being sold at fish markets and grocery stores, so you can buy packages from the freezer section without sacrificing quality. Whenever possible, look for shrimp labeled "wild-caught," and with the shells and tails intact, which will help keep the shrimp moist and plump during cooking.

Two-Ingredient Sauces

LEMON-DILL SAUCE
makes ½ cup

—

Stir together ½ cup fresh **lemon** juice (from 2 to 3 lemons) and ¼ cup coarsely chopped **fresh dill** just before serving.

SRIRACHA MAYONNAISE
makes ½ cup

—

Swirl 2 to 3 tablespoons **Sriracha** (or to taste) into ½ cup **mayonnaise** just before serving.

MISO BUTTER
makes ½ cup

—

Melt ½ cup (1 stick) unsalted **butter**. Stir in 2 tablespoons **white miso** in a bowl until smooth and combined. Miso butter can be refrigerated up to 2 weeks; rewarm before serving.

In the United States, more than 100 million pounds of avocados—all mashed into one form of guacamole or another—are eaten on Super Bowl Sunday alone. Guacamole has also become beloved every day of the year. The most traditional version has universal appeal, but even purists will appreciate the two variations here.

Guacamole

CLASSIC GUACAMOLE
makes 2 cups

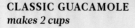

Mash 4 ripe but firm peeled and pitted **avocados** in a bowl with a fork or potato masher until chunky, then mix in 2 tablespoons fresh **lime** juice, 1 minced **jalapeño** (ribs and seeds removed if less heat is desired), ½ cup finely chopped **red onion**, and 2 tablespoons coarsely chopped **fresh cilantro** leaves. Season with **coarse salt**. Serve immediately, garnished with whole cilantro leaves and chopped red onion.

MAKE AHEAD Guacamole is best served immediately, but it can be refrigerated, with plastic wrap pressed directly onto the surface (to prevent discoloration), for several hours.

KIWI AND MINT
makes 2 cups

—

Prepare classic guacamole recipe (opposite), omitting cilantro and red onion, then fold in 2 **kiwis**, peeled and cut into ½-inch pieces, and 2 tablespoons **fresh mint** leaves (chopped if large). Serve immediately, garnished with more mint leaves.

TOMATO AND QUESO FRESCO
makes 2 cups

—

Prepare classic guacamole recipe (opposite), then season with freshly ground **pepper** and stir in ⅓ cup finely chopped and seeded **plum tomatoes**. Sprinkle with 2 tablespoons **queso fresco** or feta cheese. Serve immediately, garnished with whole cilantro leaves.

A staple at tapas bars, croquettes are creamy and crunchy all at once. They're also incredibly habit-forming. Cook them in small batches for the best results (each batch takes only about two minutes to fry), and keep them warm in the oven until ready to serve, with a Spanish red wine (such as Tempranillo or Rioja) or sherry.

Croquettes
—

makes 24

1 pound Yukon Gold potatoes, peeled and cut into ½-inch pieces

Coarse salt and freshly ground pepper

2 tablespoons unsalted butter

½ to ¾ cup milk, warmed

1 cup all-purpose flour

1 large egg

1½ cups plain fresh breadcrumbs (see page 242)

Canola oil, for frying

Flat-leaf parsley sprigs, for garnish

1. In a large pot, cover potatoes by 2 inches with water. Bring to a boil; add salt and reduce to a simmer. Cook until potatoes are fork-tender, about 12 minutes. Drain thoroughly and return to pot; mash with a fork or potato masher until smooth. Add butter and stir over low heat until melted. Continue to cook, stirring constantly, until potatoes are stiff, about 1 minute. Gradually stir in ½ cup warm milk until combined, adding up to ¼ cup more milk as needed (potato mixture should be moistened but not too thin). Let cool, then season with salt and pepper.

2. Place flour in a shallow bowl, season with salt and pepper, and whisk to combine. In another shallow bowl, whisk egg with 1 tablespoon water. Place breadcrumbs in a third shallow bowl. Form potato mixture into ¾-by-2-inch ovals. Dredge each oval in flour, shaking off excess, dip in egg wash, then roll in breadcrumbs to coat. Transfer to a parchment-lined baking sheet.

3. Heat about 1¼ inches oil in a heavy-bottomed pot over medium-high until 350°F on a deep-fry thermometer. Working in batches, fry croquettes until golden all over, about 2 minutes. Use a slotted spoon to transfer to paper towels to drain. Return oil to 350°F between batches. Serve warm, garnished with sprigs of parsley.

MAKE AHEAD The mashed potato mixture can be prepared through step 1 up to a day ahead and refrigerated, covered. You can also form and coat the ovals up to an hour ahead, and keep on a baking sheet lined with a wire rack; this can also help them become even more crisp during frying.

NOTE To keep them warm while you finish frying batches, place croquettes on a parchment-lined baking sheet in a 225°F oven.

Recipes for hot artichoke dip have been passed down for generations, yet the familiar starter is still going strong. After all, the combination of canned artichoke hearts, Parmesan, and mayonnaise is as good as it gets, though garlic, lemon juice, and scallion are added here for even more unbeatable flavor. Save some of the artichoke leaves for the top; they'll turn golden and crisp during baking. Serve with toasted bread and crunchy vegetables.

Hot Artichoke Dip

serves 10 to 12

3 cans (14 ounces each) artichoke hearts in water

6 tablespoons unsalted butter

¼ cup all-purpose flour

2 cups whole milk, warmed

⅛ teaspoon cayenne pepper

Coarse salt and freshly ground black pepper

1 cup finely grated Parmigiano-Reggiano cheese

1 cup finely grated Pecorino cheese

1 large onion, finely chopped

1 tablespoon fresh thyme leaves, chopped

3 garlic cloves, minced

1½ teaspoons finely grated lemon zest

¼ cup fresh coarse breadcrumbs (see page 242)

Assorted accompaniments, such as carrots or other crudités, and toasted bread, for serving

1. Remove leaves from 1 artichoke heart; pat dry, and reserve. Thinly slice remaining artichokes; pat dry.

2. Preheat oven to 400°F. Melt 4 tablespoons butter in a saucepan over medium heat. Add flour, and cook, stirring constantly, 2 minutes. Gradually whisk in milk, and bring to a boil. Add cayenne and season with salt and black pepper. Reduce to a simmer and cook, stirring, until thickened, about 2 minutes. Remove from heat, and stir in cheeses.

3. Melt remaining 2 tablespoons butter in a skillet over medium-high heat. Add onion, and cook 3 minutes. Add thyme, garlic, and sliced artichokes, and cook, stirring frequently, 3 minutes. Add to cheese mixture along with lemon zest. Transfer to a 2-quart baking dish.

4. Top with reserved artichoke leaves and sprinkle with breadcrumbs. Bake until golden and bubbling, about 15 minutes. Serve warm, with accompaniments.

MAKE AHEAD Dip can be prepared through step 3 up to 1 day ahead; let cool completely, cover with plastic wrap, and refrigerate. Bring to room temperature, top with artichoke leaves, and sprinkle with breadcrumbs before baking as directed.

Dates wrapped in sliced bacon and roasted to perfection are known as devils on horseback (shown opposite, second row from top), and they are just as popular now as they were back in the 1950s, when they first came on the scene. Their timeless appeal inspired four other delicious bacon-wrapped morsels (from top to bottom): peeled shrimp, plump fresh figs filled with blue cheese, cream-cheese-stuffed jalapeño chiles, and little potatoes. Everything *does* taste better with bacon, after all.

Bacon-Wrapped Bites

GINGER SHRIMP
makes 24

■

12 bacon slices (not thick-cut)

24 large shrimp (about 1½ pounds), peeled and deveined (see page 242), tails left intact

2 tablespoons low-sodium soy sauce

2 teaspoons finely grated peeled fresh ginger

1 teaspoon light-brown sugar

1. Preheat oven to 475°F, with rack on upper shelf. Halve each bacon slice crosswise. Wrap each piece around a shrimp.

2. In a bowl, whisk together soy sauce, ginger, and brown sugar until sugar is dissolved. Brush bacon-wrapped shrimp with soy-sauce mixture. Transfer to a parchment-lined rimmed baking sheet, seam side down.

3. Bake 10 minutes. Heat broiler; broil until bacon is crisp at edges and shrimp are cooked through, 2 to 3 minutes. Serve warm or at room temperature.

PISTACHIO-STUFFED DATES
makes 24

■

24 pitted dates

½ cup salted shelled pistachios

¼ cup dried apricots

12 bacon slices (not thick-cut)

1. Preheat oven to 450°F. Stuff each date with 2 to 3 pistachios. Cut dried apricots into 24 strips. Halve each bacon slice crosswise. Lay a stuffed date and apricot strip on top of each bacon slice, then wrap to enclose. Transfer to a parchment-lined rimmed baking sheet, seam side down.

2. Bake until bacon is crisp, about 10 minutes, flipping each wrapped date after 5 minutes. (If frozen, bake 10 minutes; flip, and bake 10 minutes more.) Transfer to paper towels to drain. Serve warm or at room temperature.

MAKE AHEAD Before baking, bacon-wrapped dates can be frozen on a baking sheet, wrapped in plastic, until firm, about 1 hour; transfer to a resealable plastic bag, and freeze up to 1 month. Bake straight from the freezer as directed in the recipe.

ABOUT DATES Dried dates come in many varieties, but Deglet Nour are the most commonly found pitted in the United States—and the ones used here. Look for soft, plump dates, and avoid those with sugar crystals on their skin, which indicate they are past their prime. Store them in a cool, dark place for up to 6 months, or in the refrigerator for up to 1 year.

Bacon-Wrapped Bites

BLUE CHEESE—STUFFED FIGS
makes 24

- 6 bacon slices (not thick-cut)
- 24 ripe but firm fresh figs
- 4 ounces creamy blue cheese, such as gorgonzola dolce

1. Preheat oven to 375°F. Halve each bacon slice crosswise, then lengthwise. Cook bacon in a large skillet over medium-low heat until bacon is just golden but still pliable, and some of fat is rendered, 3 to 4 minutes. Transfer to paper towels to drain and let cool.

2. Cut a deep X in the side of each fig. Lightly squeeze figs from top and bottom to open X's, then stuff each with 1 teaspoon blue cheese. Press on X's to enclose cheese, then wrap each fig with a piece of bacon. Transfer figs to a parchment-lined rimmed baking sheet.

3. Bake until figs are warmed through and bacon is crisp, about 5 minutes. Serve warm or at room temperature.

CREAM-CHEESE-STUFFED JALAPEÑOS
makes 24

- 12 bacon slices (not thick-cut)
- 12 large chile peppers, such as jalapeño or Fresno
- 1 bar (8 ounces) cream cheese, room temperature

1. Preheat oven to 375°F. Halve each bacon slice crosswise. Halve chile peppers lengthwise, then remove ribs and seeds. Dividing evenly, fill chile halves with cream cheese; wrap each with a piece of bacon. Transfer to a parchment-lined rimmed baking sheet, stuffed side up.

2. Bake until bacon is crisp at the edges, 18 to 20 minutes. Serve warm or at room temperature.

BACON-WRAPPED POTATOES
makes 24

- 12 bacon slices
- 24 small (1-inch-diameter) potatoes

1. Preheat oven to 375°F. Halve each bacon slice crosswise. Wrap each piece around a potato and secure with a toothpick. Transfer to a parchment-lined rimmed baking sheet.

2. Bake until bacon is crisp and potatoes are tender when pierced with the tip of a sharp knife, 40 to 50 minutes. Transfer to paper towels to drain. Serve warm.

Here's an all-time favorite: Sprinkle bacon slices with sugar—in this case, raw turbinado sugar, but brown sugar works well, too—and then bake until burnished with a glistening glaze. Cut into bite-size morsels, they are the ultimate partner for cocktails.

Glazed–Bacon Bites

—

Makes about 30 pieces

- 1 **pound thick-cut bacon, room temperature**
- ¼ **cup raw turbinado or dark-brown sugar (packed)**
- 2 **teaspoons fresh thyme leaves**

1. Preheat oven to 350°F. Line a rimmed baking sheet with parchment and set a wire rack on top. Lay bacon slices on rack, then sprinkle with sugar, spreading to coat evenly and pressing to adhere. Let rest in a warm spot until sugar begins to dissolve, about 10 minutes.

2. Bake until bacon is crisp and evenly glazed, flipping slices halfway through, 25 to 35 minutes, sprinkling with thyme during last 5 minutes of baking. Remove from oven; when cool enough to handle, cut bacon crosswise into thirds, and keep in a warm spot until ready to serve.

Onion dips have a long history among American home cooks, perhaps none as well-known (or beloved) as the one made famous by the soup mix. This version takes the starter to a different level, with the flavor of caramelized onions mingling with the equally delectable taste of crisp bacon. Fried shallot rings are an optional garnish, but they cook in mere minutes and add another winning dimension to the dish.

Caramelized Onion and Bacon Dip

serves 8

2 tablespoons extra-virgin olive oil

3 pounds yellow onions (about 8 large), halved and thinly sliced

Coarse salt and freshly ground pepper

¼ cup red-wine vinegar

1 tablespoon chopped fresh thyme leaves

4 slices bacon, chopped

1 bar (8 ounces) cream cheese, room temperature

1 cup sour cream

Safflower oil, for frying

4 shallots, thinly sliced into rings

NOTE You can caramelize a few batches of onions all at once, days ahead of time, and refrigerate until ready to make the dip. Use extras for tarts (such as the one on page 80), crostini, frittatas, and pizza.

1. Heat olive oil in a medium heavy-bottomed pot over medium-high until hot but not smoking. Cook onions, stirring occasionally, until soft and golden, about 15 minutes. Cover; reduce heat to low. Cook, stirring occasionally, until browned and caramelized, about 40 minutes.

2. Raise heat to medium, and season onions with salt. Stir in vinegar; simmer until mixture is dry. Stir in thyme; remove from heat. Let cool slightly, then coarsely chop onions.

3. Meanwhile, cook bacon in a small skillet, stirring occasionally, until fat has been rendered, 3 to 4 minutes. Using a slotted spoon, transfer bacon to paper towels to drain.

4. Beat cream cheese in a bowl until smooth. Fold in sour cream and caramelized onions; season with salt and pepper. Refrigerate, covered, at least 1 hour.

5. Heat ¼ inch safflower oil in a small sauté pan over medium until shimmering. Working in 3 batches, fry shallots, stirring occasionally, until golden brown, about 2 minutes. Use a slotted spoon to transfer to paper towels to drain; season with salt. Garnish dip with shallots and serve.

MAKE AHEAD The dip can be refrigerated, covered, up to 3 days; top with fried shallots just before serving. Fried shallots will keep up to 1 week at room temperature in an airtight container.

Don't let the lengthy list of ingredients deter you from making this recipe. Pickling boiled shrimp requires very little extra effort—just combine everything in a tightly sealed jar, shake to distribute, and chill. The shrimp are a perfect match for martinis (page 238), and you might also want to bake a batch of Southern-Style Cheese Straws (page 100) to serve alongside.

Pickled Shrimp

serves 6 to 8

1 teaspoon Old Bay seasoning

1 dried bay leaf

1 tablespoon plus 1 teaspoon coarse salt

1 pound small shrimp (40 to 50 count), peeled and deveined (see page 242; leave tails intact, if desired)

1 cup extra-virgin olive oil

⅓ cup fresh lemon juice

⅓ cup cider vinegar

¼ cup chopped fresh flat-leaf parsley leaves

½ teaspoon red-pepper flakes

2 garlic cloves, minced

½ yellow onion, thinly sliced

1 teaspoon mustard seeds

¼ teaspoon whole cloves

¼ teaspoon juniper berries

½ teaspoon celery seeds

1. In a pot, bring 2 quarts water, the Old Bay seasoning, bay leaf, and 1 tablespoon salt to a boil. Reduce heat and simmer 10 minutes. Add shrimp and cook until just pink and opaque, about 30 seconds; drain.

2. Stir together shrimp and remaining ingredients in a large bowl. Transfer mixture to an airtight container. Cover tightly; shake to distribute. Refrigerate at least 8 hours before serving.

MAKE AHEAD Shrimp can be allowed to marinate up to 1 week in the refrigerator; shake to distribute again just before serving.

How to update the classic baked brie? Cook it on the grill for an unmistakable smoky flavor. You can use other types of soft, creamy cheese, too, like Camembert, as long as the wheel has a thick rind and an inside that's soft but not too runny. Serve with grilled baguette slices and tomato jam (or store-bought fruit chutney, in a pinch).

Grilled Brie with Tomato Jam

—

serves 6 to 8

1 wheel Brie (about 8 ounces)
   Extra-virgin olive oil, for brushing
1 baguette, sliced ¼-inch thick on the bias
   Tomato Jam (recipe follows), for serving

1. Heat grill (or grill pan) to high, with an area for indirect heat. (If using a charcoal grill, leave a third of the grill free of briquettes; the coals are ready when you can hold the palm of your hand 6 inches above the grates for just 2 to 3 seconds.)

2. Brush hot grates and the cheese rind with oil. Grill until cheese is marked by grates on the outside and starting to melt inside, flipping once, about 3 minutes per side.

3. Meanwhile, brush baguette slices with oil on both sides. Grill, flipping once, until marked by grates, about 1 minute per side. Serve with cheese and jam.

TOMATO JAM
makes 1½ cups

—

1 tablespoon extra-virgin olive oil
2 small garlic cloves, minced
1 piece (1 inch) fresh ginger, peeled and minced (1 tablespoon)
1 small red onion, finely chopped
1 can (28 ounces) whole peeled tomatoes in juice
½ cup red-wine vinegar
¼ cup honey
¼ cup packed light-brown sugar
½ teaspoon ground ginger
   Pinch of ground cloves
2 cinnamon sticks

1. Heat oil in a medium saucepan over medium. Add garlic, fresh ginger, and onion, and cook, stirring frequently, until softened, about 5 minutes. Add tomatoes and their juices, breaking up tomatoes with a wooden spoon. Add vinegar, honey, brown sugar, ground ginger, cloves, and cinnamon.

2. Bring to a simmer and cook, stirring occasionally, until tomatoes have completely broken down and mixture is thick, 60 to 75 minutes. Discard cinnamon. Let cool completely before serving or storing. Tomato jam can be refrigerated in an airtight container up to 2 weeks.

This quick take on the Provençal pizza-like tart known as pissadalière is topped by sautéed onions, slivered Niçoise olives, fresh thyme, and anchovies. Puff pastry makes a fast and easy alternative to traditional bread or pastry doughs when making it or other tarts: Once the sheets have thawed, roll them out and sprinkle with your choice of toppings, then pop in the oven and you're done.

Provençal Onion Tart

serves 8 to 10

1 tablespoon unsalted butter

2 tablespoons extra-virgin olive oil

2 onions, thinly sliced

2 tablespoons fresh thyme leaves

   All-purpose flour, for dusting

1 sheet frozen puff pastry, preferably all-butter (see note, page 57), thawed

¼ cup oil-cured small black olives, pitted and halved lengthwise

4 to 6 anchovy fillets, preferably salt-packed, rinsed (optional)

1. Preheat oven to 425°F. Melt butter with oil in a medium skillet over medium-high heat. Add onions and thyme, and cook, stirring occasionally, until onions are golden and soft, about 10 minutes.

2. On a lightly floured surface, roll out pastry to an 8½-by-15-inch rectangle, trimming edges to make them straight. Place on a parchment-lined baking sheet, transfer to oven, and immediately reduce oven temperature to 400°F. Bake until pastry just begins to puff, about 12 minutes.

3. Arrange onions in a single layer over pastry, leaving a 1-inch border all around. Top with olives and anchovies (if desired). Bake 15 minutes. Reduce oven temperature to 375°F, and continue baking until tart is puffed and golden around the edges, about 15 minutes more (tent with foil if crust browns too quickly). Let cool slightly before cutting into small squares and serving.

It's hard to resist the appeal of tucking into a bowl of creamy dip. The ones here can be made ahead, meaning one less thing to labor over when you're the host. Consider any of these vegetable-based options as a healthier alternative to dairy-laden dips. Serve them with crackers or bread, or spoon them into endive spears or celery hearts. Eating your vegetables has never been this much fun.

Pureed Vegetable Dips

CAULIFLOWER-SPINACH DIP
makes about 2 cups

—

Arrange 4 cups **cauliflower** florets (from 1 head) in a steamer basket (or colander) set in a saucepan filled with 2 inches water; bring to a boil, then reduce to a simmer. Cover and steam until florets are tender, about 8 minutes. Add 2 cups lightly packed **spinach** leaves to basket and cook, covered, just until wilted, about 2 minutes.

Transfer mixture to a food processor, and add 3 tablespoons each **tahini**, fresh **lemon** juice, and 3 tablespoons **extra-virgin olive oil**, and 1 smashed small **garlic** clove. Season with **coarse salt** and freshly ground **pepper**. Process until smooth. Serve at room temperature.

ROASTED BEET DIP
makes about 2 cups

—

Preheat oven to 375°F. Place 3 **beets** (1 pound), trimmed and scrubbed, on a piece of foil lined with parchment. Drizzle with 1 tablespoon **extra-virgin olive oil**, season with **coarse salt**, and toss to combine. Fold foil to form a packet, crimping edges to seal, and place on a baking sheet. Roast until beets are tender, about 1 hour. Let beets cool slightly, then rub off skins using paper towels and cut into quarters.

Transfer beets to a food processor. Add 1 tablespoon **pomegranate molasses**, 1 tablespoon extra-virgin olive oil, and ¼ teaspoon ground **cinnamon**. Process until smooth. Add more molasses, if desired, to taste. Serve at room temperature.

SPICED CARROT DIP
makes about 2 cups

—

Peel and thinly slice 10 medium **carrots** (1 pound). Arrange in a steamer basket (or colander) set in a saucepan filled with 2 inches water; bring to a boil, then reduce to a simmer. Cover and steam until carrots are tender, about 12 minutes.

Transfer carrots to a food processor, and add ½ smashed small **garlic** clove, ¼ teaspoon ground **cumin**, ¼ teaspoon finely grated peeled **fresh ginger**, ⅛ teaspoon ground **cinnamon**, a pinch of **cayenne pepper**, 1 tablespoon **tahini**, and 2 teaspoons fresh **lemon** juice. Season with **coarse salt** and freshly ground **black pepper**. Process until smooth, adding up to 2 tablespoons water, if necessary, to reach desired consistency. Serve at room temperature.

MAKE AHEAD The dips can be refrigerated, covered, up to 3 days. Bring to room temperature before serving.

These Japanese beef-and-asparagus bundles will deliver style and substance to any pre-dinner scene. After some initial prep work—blanching the asparagus, pounding the meat to a uniform thinness, rolling up the vegetables in the steak—negimaki take just two minutes to grill (or broil). Serve with Rye Derby cocktails (page 239).

Beef and Asparagus Negimaki

—

makes 24

48 thin stalks asparagus, or 24 thick stalks sliced in half lengthwise

Coarse salt and freshly ground pepper

1 cup low-sodium soy sauce

½ cup sugar

1½ pounds beef tenderloin, cut into 24 ¼-inch-thick slices

1 bunch scallions, pale- and dark-green parts cut into 3½-inch lengths

1. Heat a grill (or grill pan) to medium-high. (If using a charcoal grill, coals are ready when you can hold your hand 6 inches above grate for just 3 to 4 seconds.)

2. Trim asparagus tips to 3½-inch lengths; reserve bottoms for another use. Blanch tips in a pot of boiling salted water until bright green and just tender, about 1 minute. Drain asparagus; transfer to an ice-water bath to cool. Drain again.

3. Whisk together soy sauce and sugar in a small bowl until sugar is dissolved; reserve half of sauce mixture in another bowl (for serving).

4. Place one beef slice between two pieces of plastic wrap; use a meat mallet or heavy skillet to pound lightly to an even thickness. Remove plastic; trim to a 2-by-5-inch rectangle. Repeat with remaining beef.

5. Dip a piece of beef in soy-sauce mixture, and place on a clean surface. Season with pepper. Place 1 piece of scallion and 2 asparagus tips across 1 end of beef, so vegetables extend over edges; roll up. Repeat with remaining beef and vegetables.

6. Arrange on grill, seam side down; cook, brushing negimaki with sauce and turning, until slightly charred in spots, about 2 minutes for medium-rare. Serve warm, with reserved sauce.

NOTE The negimaki can also be broiled: Heat broiler with rack 4 inches from heat source. Arrange rolls on a rimmed baking sheet, seam side down. Broil, brushing with sauce and turning, until charred, about 2 minutes.

MAKE AHEAD You can blanch the asparagus and pound the beef several hours ahead; store separately, covered, in the refrigerator. The rolls can be assembled an hour in advance and kept at room temperature.

Using wonton wrappers instead of pasta dough eases the preparation of this savory starter, and results in a crisp, light crust. The ravioli are also a great make-ahead option; reheat in the oven when ready to serve, as a toasty prelude to a cold-weather meal.

Fried Sweet-Potato Ravioli

makes 38

3 sweet potatoes, scrubbed

¼ cup heavy cream

¼ cup finely grated Parmigiano-Reggiano cheese

Coarse salt and freshly ground pepper

38 square wonton wrappers

1 large egg whisked with 1 tablespoon water, for egg wash

Safflower oil, for frying

Sour cream and snipped fresh chives, for serving

1. Preheat oven to 400°F. Prick sweet potatoes all over with a fork. Roast on a rimmed baking sheet until tender, about 1 hour. When cool enough to handle, scoop out flesh and transfer to a food processor. Pulse with heavy cream and cheese until smooth. Season with salt and pepper.

2. Working with one wonton wrapper at a time, place 2 teaspoons sweet potato filling in center of square. Lightly brush edges of wrapper with egg wash. Lightly press edges to seal. Using a small knife, make small decorative cuts along edges, if desired. Transfer ravioli to a parchment-lined baking sheet and cover with a kitchen towel.

3. Heat 2 inches oil in a heavy-bottomed pot over medium-high until 350°F on a deep-fry thermometer. Line a wire rack with paper towels. Working in batches, cook ravioli until golden on the bottom, 1 to 2 minutes; flip and cook until other side is golden, 1 to 2 minutes more. Use a slotted spoon to transfer to lined rack to drain. Return oil to 350°F between batches. Serve immediately with sour cream topped with chives.

MAKE AHEAD Arrange cooked and cooled ravioli in a single layer on a rimmed baking sheet. Freeze until firm. Transfer to a resealable plastic bag and freeze up to 3 months. Reheat on a parchment-lined baking sheet (do not thaw) in a 375°F oven, about 10 minutes.

NOTE To keep them warm while you finish frying batches, place ravioli on a parchment-lined baking sheet in a 225°F oven.

Fondue, Mexican-style: It's as easy as the celebrated Swiss dish, but with just a few tweaks. First, sauté onions and chiles in a skillet, add a splash of tequila (you'll have plenty left over for making margaritas), then stir in shredded Monterey Jack until melted. Serve with sliced chorizo and tortilla chips.

Queso Fundido with Chorizo

serves 6 to 8

2 tablespoons extra-virgin olive oil

1 pound Spanish (cured) chorizo, sliced on the bias ⅜ inch thick

1 cup finely chopped sweet onion, such as Vidalia

1 can (4 ounces) diced green chiles

Coarse salt

⅓ cup tequila, preferably gold

4 cups shredded Monterey Jack cheese (1 pound)

Tortilla chips, for serving

1. Heat oil in a large, heavy skillet (preferably cast iron) over medium. Working in batches, add chorizo and cook, stirring occasionally, until browned in spots, 3 to 4 minutes. Transfer chorizo to a serving dish.

2. Add onion and chiles to skillet, and season with salt; raise heat to medium-high. Sauté, stirring occasionally, until onion is translucent, about 5 minutes. Add tequila, bring to a boil, and cook until tequila is mostly evaporated, about 30 seconds.

3. Reduce heat to low, gradually stir in cheese, and cook, stirring constantly, just until cheese is melted, 5 to 7 minutes. Transfer to a fondue pot (see note, below) and serve immediately with chips and chorizo.

NOTE You can serve Queso Fundido in the skillet it is cooked in if you don't have a fondue pot; return it to the stove and warm over low heat if needed.

If you're happy when guests congregate near the kitchen, consider serving fritto misto, or "fried mix," at your next dinner party. This way, they can enjoy each batch as soon as it's ready. Here, thinly sliced artichokes, fennel, lemons, and parsley are tossed with buttermilk, then coated with flour and fried to a golden-brown crust. We think fritto misto tastes best with prosecco, but any crisp, dry Italian white wine (try Orvieto or Verdicchio) is also nice.

Artichoke, Fennel, and Lemon Fritto Misto

Serves 10

2 medium artichokes

1 large fennel bulb, trimmed, halved, and thinly sliced crosswise

2 lemons, washed and very thinly sliced into rounds

2 cups buttermilk

½ cup fresh flat-leaf parsley leaves

3 cups all-purpose flour

Coarse salt and freshly ground pepper

Safflower oil, for frying

1. To separate artichoke bottoms, slice off upper two-thirds of each bulb and discard. Snap off tough outer leaves; scoop out choke with a spoon. Use a vegetable peeler or paring knife to remove green outer layer from around heart and stem. Thinly slice bottoms lengthwise.

2. In a bowl, stir together artichoke bottoms, fennel, lemons, and buttermilk to coat evenly. Place flour in another bowl; season with salt and pepper, and whisk to combine.

3. Heat 2 inches oil in a heavy deep-sided skillet over medium-high until 370°F on a deep-fry thermometer. Use a slotted spoon to transfer vegetables and lemons to a sieve to drain. Place parsley in bowl with buttermilk, then drain and discard liquid.

4. Working in batches of 6 to 7 pieces at a time, dredge each vegetable and lemon slice in seasoned flour, then carefully place in the hot oil. Cook until golden brown, flipping once, about 3 minutes total. Use a slotted spoon to transfer to paper towels to drain. (Return oil to 370°F between batches.) Dredge parsley in flour, then fry until golden, about 30 seconds. Drain on paper towels. As soon as each batch is done, sprinkle with salt and serve immediately.

Minimal prep time *and* maximum flavor: That's why you'll want to serve these Thai-inspired skewers over and over again. Half of the five-ingredient sauce is brushed on the shrimp as they grill, and the rest is served alongside, for dipping. The shrimp are great with cold beer and tropical cocktails, such as Ginger Caipirinhas (page 234) or Pom Sunrises (page 238).

Spicy Shrimp Skewers

—

serves 12

½ cup sugar

1 teaspoon finely grated lime zest, plus ¼ cup fresh lime juice (from 2 to 3 limes)

1 tablespoon Asian chili paste, such as sambal oelek

1 tablespoon fish sauce, such as nam pla

Coarse salt

Safflower oil, for brushing

36 large shrimp (about 2 pounds), peeled and deveined (see page 242; tails left intact, if desired)

1. Bring sugar and lime juice to a simmer in a saucepan. Cook, stirring, until sugar dissolves, about 2 minutes. Remove from heat; stir in lime zest, chili paste, and fish sauce. Season with salt. Transfer half of sauce to another bowl (for serving).

2. Heat grill (or grill pan) to high. (If using a charcoal grill, coals are ready when you can hold the palm of your hand 6 inches above grates for just 2 to 3 seconds.) Thread 2 shrimp onto each skewer; season with salt.

3. Brush grates with oil. Grill shrimp for 1 minute; brush with some of sauce. Flip and grill for 1 minute more; brush with sauce again. Flip and grill, brushing occasionally with sauce, until opaque, 1 to 2 minutes more. Serve with reserved sauce.

NOTE You can also broil the shrimp skewers: Heat broiler with rack 4 inches from heat source. Arrange skewers on a rimmed baking sheet, brush with some sauce, and cook 2 minutes. Flip, brush with more sauce, and grill until opaque and browned in spots, about 2 minutes more.

TIP If using wooden skewers, soak them in water for about 30 minutes to keep them from scorching on the grill (or under the broiler).

This scaled-down version of flautas—the crisp deep-fried wonders of Mexican restaurants—is even better than the full-size originals. They are certainly easier to eat (in just two bites) without losing any of the deeply flavorful chicken-and-cheese filling. Fresh Tomatillo Salsa, Pico de Gallo, and Salsa de Árbol (all are on page 31) are other good alternatives to the one here, used in the filling and for serving.

Mini Chicken Flautas

—

makes 32

2 boneless, skinless chicken breast halves (about 8 ounces each)

2 teaspoons chipotle-chile powder

Coarse salt

1 tablespoon safflower oil, plus more for frying

½ cup crumbled cotija cheese or feta cheese

¾ cup Fire-Roasted Salsa (recipe follows), plus more for serving

16 corn tortillas (6 inch), warmed (see note, below)

1. Sprinkle chicken with chipotle powder, and season with salt. Heat oil in a sauté pan over medium-high. Add chicken; cook until golden and cooked through, 5 to 6 minutes per side. Transfer to a cutting board; when cool enough to handle, shred chicken with a fork. In a bowl, toss with cheese and salsa; season with salt.

2. Working with one warm tortilla at a time (keep the rest covered), place 2 tablespoons filling in a line down center of tortilla. Roll up tightly. Secure rolls on both ends with toothpicks. Slice in half; transfer to a rimmed baking sheet, and cover with a kitchen towel. Repeat with remaining tortillas.

3. Heat 2 inches oil in a heavy-bottomed pot over medium-high until 350°F on a deep-fry thermometer. Line a wire rack with paper towels. Working in batches, cook flautas, turning once, until golden, about 3 minutes. Transfer to lined rack with a slotted spoon. Remove toothpicks. Serve immediately, with salsa.

FIRE-ROASTED SALSA
makes 2 cups

—

2 jalapeño chiles

3 garlic cloves (unpeeled)

1 can (15 ounces) diced fire-roasted tomatoes

½ cup diced white onion

½ cup fresh cilantro leaves, chopped

1 tablespoon fresh lime juice

Coarse salt and freshly ground pepper

1. Toast jalapeños and garlic cloves in a dry cast-iron skillet over medium-high heat, turning occasionally, until softened and charred, about 8 minutes. Remove and let cool. Remove stem (and ribs and seeds for less heat, if desired) from jalapeños, and peel garlic.

2. Transfer jalapeños and garlic to a food processor; add diced tomatoes and juices. Pulse until combined but still chunky. Add onion, cilantro, and lime juice, and pulse just until combined. Season with salt and pepper. Salsa can be refrigerated, covered, up to 1 week before using.

NOTE To warm tortillas, stack 4 on parchment-lined foil and wrap to enclose. Heat in 350°F oven 15 minutes. Or stack 5 tortillas on a plate, cover with a damp paper towel, and microwave just until warm, about 30 seconds.

MAKE AHEAD Freeze cooked flautas on a rimmed baking sheet until firm, 1 hour. Transfer to a reseal-able plastic bag; freeze up to 3 months. Reheat (without thawing) on a parchment-lined baking sheet in 375°F oven, 10 minutes.

Celebrate the arrival of spring with garden-fresh artichokes and a trio of dipping sauces. Steaming is by far the easiest way to prepare the globes—all it takes is minimal trimming and snipping to get them ready, then some hands-off cooking for a half-hour or so to reach the proper tenderness. The sauces are also a cinch to make—even the hollandaise, thanks to the blender. Serve with a crisp, dry white wine such as Sancerre, or with our Meyer Lemon Drops (page 238).

Steamed Artichokes
—

makes 4

4 large artichokes

1 lemon, halved

Coarse salt

Dipping Sauces (recipes follow)

1. Working with one artichoke at a time, snap off tough outer leaves. Using a serrated knife, cut off top one third of artichokes and discard. Snip remaining sharp or spiky tips, using kitchen shears. Trim stems so artichokes stand upright. Rub cut surfaces with lemon to prevent discoloration.

2. Set a steamer basket (or colander) in a large pot filled with enough water so it reaches just below basket. Squeeze lemon juice from lemon halves into water, and add a generous amount of salt; bring to a boil. Place artichokes in basket, stemmed-side up. Cover and steam until artichoke hearts are knife-tender and inner leaves pull out easily, 25 to 35 minutes; add more water to pot, as necessary. Serve warm or at room temperature, with dipping sauces.

Dipping Sauces

BLENDER HOLLANDAISE
makes about 1½ cups
—

Combine 3 large **egg** yolks, 2 tablespoons fresh **lemon** juice, ½ teaspoon **coarse salt**, and a pinch of **cayenne pepper** in a blender. With motor running, slowly add ¾ cup (1½ sticks) melted, cooled unsalted **butter**. Transfer sauce to a bowl; if too thick, whisk in warm water, 1 tablespoon at a time. Sauce can be kept in a bowl set over a pan of simmering water, up to 1 hour.

LEMON-SHALLOT BUTTER
makes about 1 cup
—

Melt ½ cup (1 stick) unsalted **butter** in a saucepan over medium-high heat. Add 2 minced **shallots** and the finely grated zest of 1 **lemon**. Cook, stirring frequently, until shallot is softened, about 2 minutes. Reduce heat to medium. Whisk in juice of 1 lemon. Serve warm.

MUSTARD VINAIGRETTE
makes about 1⅓ cups
—

In a small bowl, whisk together 2 tablespoons **Dijon mustard** and ⅓ cup **champagne vinegar**. Slowly add 1 cup **extra-virgin olive oil** in a steady stream, whisking constantly until dressing is creamy and emulsified. Season with **coarse salt** and freshly ground **pepper**.

Two Southern favorites—hot crab dip and pimiento cheese—are better than one, especially when they are combined to create a delightfully creamy appetizer. Making the spread couldn't be simpler: The ingredients are quickly mixed together, then it takes less than a half-hour to bake until golden, bubbling, and ready to serve with chips and crudités. A pre-dinner winner, if ever there was one.

Hot-Crab and Pimiento-Cheese Spread

—

Serves 8 to 10

1　bar (8 ounces) cream cheese, room temperature

6　ounces extra-sharp yellow cheddar cheese, shredded (about 2 cups)

½　cup plus 2 tablespoons mayonnaise

8　ounces jumbo lump crabmeat, picked over

¼　cup chopped pimiento (from a 4-ounce jar)

¼　cup sliced scallions (from about 3 scallions)

1　tablespoon plus 1 teaspoon fresh lemon juice, plus more to taste

½　teaspoon coarse salt

　　Hot sauce (such as Tabasco)

1½　cups torn rustic bread (from 1 loaf, crust removed)

　　Assorted accompaniments, such as cucumber spears, endive leaves, and potato chips

1. Preheat oven to 375°F. Mash cream cheese in a bowl until very soft. Add cheddar and ½ cup mayonnaise and stir to combine. Stir in crab, pimiento, scallions, lemon juice, salt, and hot sauce to taste. Spoon mixture into a 2-quart baking dish.

2. Stir together torn bread and remaining 2 tablespoons mayonnaise in a bowl, then sprinkle over spread. Bake on a baking sheet until golden brown and bubbling, about 25 minutes. Serve immediately with accompaniments.

MAKE AHEAD Spread can be prepared through step 1 up to 1 day ahead; transfer to baking dish, and let cool completely. Remove from refrigerator 30 minutes before baking.

Not to be confused with Puff Pastry Cheese Straws (page 57), these crisp, sturdy straws are made from a rich dough that comes together quickly in a food processor. The "crackers" are traditionally piped into logs with a cookie press, which is the easiest method to use, but see the tip below for an alternate method if you don't have one. Serve cheese straws with Mint Juleps (page 235), especially on the first Saturday in May, when the horses race in Louisville, Kentucky.

Southern-Style Cheese Straws

—

makes about 24

1½ cups all-purpose flour, plus more for dusting

1 teaspoon mustard powder

1 teaspoon coarse salt

⅛ teaspoon cayenne pepper

½ cup (1 stick) unsalted butter, cut into small pieces, room temperature

1¼ cups shredded sharp cheddar cheese

MAKE AHEAD Cheese straws can be stored in an airtight container at room temperature up to 2 weeks.

1. Preheat oven to 375°F. Whisk together flour, mustard powder, salt, and cayenne in a bowl. In a food processor, pulse butter, cheese, and flour mixture just until a dough forms.

2. Divide dough into 4 equal pieces. Fit a cookie press with the ribbon disk, and fill with one portion of dough. Press dough in a continuous line onto a baking sheet (about 12 inches long). Cut into 3-inch lengths. Arrange strips 1 to 2 inches apart on a parchment-lined baking sheet. Repeat with remaining dough. Refrigerate until firm, about 15 minutes.

3. Bake until golden and firm to the touch, rotating sheets halfway through, 10 to 12 minutes. Transfer to a wire rack to cool completely.

TIP If you don't have a cookie press, wrap each quarter of dough in plastic and chill 30 minutes. Roll out each piece on a floured surface ⅛ inch thick, and cut into 1-inch-wide and 3-inch-long strips with a pastry wheel or sharp knife. Drag the tines of a fork across tops to make ridges. Chill and bake as directed.

These one-bite treats are more like savory biscuits than meatballs since you start by making a dough (with a little kick from cayenne) and then add grated cheddar and onion, ground sausage, and melted butter. The best part? They can be formed and frozen months in advance. That they're incredibly popular is yet another reason to bake a big batch.

Sausage and Cheddar Balls

—

makes 45

1¼ cups all-purpose flour

½ teaspoon coarse salt

¼ teaspoon freshly ground black pepper

½ teaspoon cayenne pepper

1½ teaspoons baking powder

2 cups grated cheddar cheese

1 pound loose breakfast sausage (or links, removed from casings)

½ large yellow onion, grated on large holes of a box grater

3 tablespoons unsalted butter, melted

1. Preheat oven to 400°F. In a large bowl, whisk together flour, salt, black pepper, cayenne pepper, and baking powder. Add cheddar and toss to coat. Add sausage, onion, and butter. With your hands, mix until well combined and then roll mixture into 1-inch balls.

2. Place balls, ½ inch apart, on parchment-lined rimmed baking sheets. Bake until golden and cooked through, rotating sheets halfway through, about 25 minutes. Serve warm.

MAKE AHEAD You can form the balls and freeze on the baking sheet until firm, about 1 hour, then transfer to resealable plastic bags and freeze up to 3 months. Bake as directed (do not thaw) for about 30 minutes.

It is impossible to eat just one of these little Greek pastries, with their savory spinach-feta filling and flaky crust. Phyllo dough is easy to use (just be sure to keep the sheets covered as you work). And the triangles can be formed and frozen ahead, then baked when ready to serve. Spanakopita is great on its own, but it's even better with Warmed Olives (page 40), or as part of a traditional mezze platter (pages 140 to 143).

Spanakopita Triangles

makes 30

5   bunches spinach (about 3½ pounds total), trimmed and washed (see tip, below)

1   tablespoon extra-virgin olive oil

2   large leeks, white and pale-green parts only, halved lengthwise, sliced crosswise, washed well and drained

2   garlic cloves, minced

    Coarse salt and freshly ground pepper

¼   teaspoon freshly grated nutmeg

¾   cup crumbled feta cheese

1   package (17.3 ounces) frozen phyllo dough, thawed

1   cup (2 sticks) unsalted butter, melted and kept warm

TIP You can substitute 12 ounces (from 2 packages) frozen spinach for the fresh, and omit step 1. Thaw as directed on package, then squeeze out extra moisture.

MAKE AHEAD Spanakopita can be prepared through step 4 up to 3 months ahead (do not brush formed triangles with butter); freeze until firm, then transfer to resealable plastic bags. To proceed, brush with butter and bake, without thawing, as directed in the recipe.

1. In a large skillet, heat ¼ cup water over medium-high. Working in batches, add spinach and cook, tossing, until completely wilted, 6 to 8 minutes. Transfer to a colander to drain, pressing out as much water as possible. Wipe skillet clean.

2. Return skillet to medium heat, and add oil. Cook leeks until softened, stirring occasionally, 6 to 8 minutes. Stir in garlic, season with salt and pepper, and cook until fragrant, about 1 minute. Stir in nutmeg. Transfer mixture to a food processor; add spinach and pulse until coarsely chopped. Transfer to a bowl. Fold in feta.

3. Preheat oven to 375°F, with racks in upper and lower thirds. On a clean work surface, lay stack of phyllo sheets flat between damp paper towels. Place one sheet flat on work surface, leaving remaining sheets covered to prevent them from drying out as you work. Brush with melted butter. Place a second phyllo sheet on top; brush with butter. Cut lengthwise into four strips, each about 3 inches wide.

4. Working with one strip at a time, place 2 tablespoons spinach mixture at one end, in a corner. Fold corner over to form a small triangle. Fold the triangle over again onto dough; continue folding until strip is rolled into a layered triangle. Trim excess with a paring knife to form a neat triangle. Brush triangle with butter; place on a parchment-lined baking sheet. Repeat process with remaining strips and dough.

5. Bake until golden, rotating sheets halfway through, 20 to 25 minutes. Transfer to wire racks. Serve warm or at room temperature.

Whenever you see squash blossoms—and fresh basil—in abundance at the greenmarket or farm stand, consider preparing a batch of these beauties. The flowers are not as delicate as they might seem, and are traditionally filled with cheese and then pan-fried. Ours are stuffed with ricotta, bocconcini, and basil; the cornmeal coating produces a light, crisp, flavorful crust. Serve with a bracing cocktail, such as the one pictured here, made with Lillet (a French fortified wine aperitif) and more basil (see page 237 for the recipe).

Fried Stuffed Squash Blossoms

—

makes 10

¾ cup fresh ricotta cheese

   Coarse salt and freshly ground pepper

10 large fresh basil leaves

1 bocconcini ball, cut into 10 pieces

10 squash blossoms

   Safflower oil, for frying

2 large eggs, lightly beaten

½ cup fine yellow cornmeal

1. Put ricotta in a fine sieve set over a bowl. Let drain in refrigerator 3 hours or overnight. Discard liquid.

2. Season ricotta with ½ teaspoon each salt and pepper; stir until smooth. Transfer to a large pastry bag fitted with a coupler. Pipe 1 scant tablespoon ricotta onto each basil leaf, then top with a piece of bocconcini. Fold leaves around cheese and pinch to close. Carefully open squash blossoms and place stuffed basil leaves inside, pressing gently to seal.

3. Heat about 3 inches oil in a heavy-bottomed saucepan over medium-high until 365°F on a deep-fry thermometer. Meanwhile, place eggs and cornmeal in separate shallow bowls. Dip each stuffed blossom into the eggs, then into the cornmeal to coat.

4. Working in batches of 2 to 3, carefully place in hot oil and cook until golden, flipping once, about 45 seconds per side. Transfer to paper towels using a slotted spoon to drain. Season with salt. Return oil to 365°F between batches. Serve immediately.

Do cheese and crackers one better: Italian Robiola Bosina cheese (also known as *due latte*, or two milks) is made from a blend of cow's and sheep's milks and is prized for its silky-smooth texture and rich, sweet taste. Here, the cheese is melted in the oven, topped with an olive-raisin relish, and served with ultra-thin and crisp flatbreads flecked with fresh herbs and sea salt. You could substitute store-bought flatbreads in a pinch, but the homemade version makes this starter that much more special—and memorable.

Warm Robiola Cheese with Pine Nuts, Olives, and Golden Raisins

—

serves 10 to 12

½ cup chopped roasted red peppers (see page 242)

2 tablespoons pine nuts, lightly toasted (see page 242)

2 tablespoons finely chopped oil-cured black olives

2 tablespoons finely chopped golden raisins

1 tablespoon finely chopped fresh oregano leaves

1 tablespoon extra-virgin olive oil

8 ounces Robiola Bosina cheese, room temperature

1. In a bowl, mix together red peppers, pine nuts, olives, raisins, oregano, and oil. Let relish stand 30 minutes.

2. Preheat oven to 375°F. Bake cheese in an ovenproof serving dish until very soft and melting around edges, 5 to 7 minutes. Top with relish. Serve immediately, with flatbread.

TIP Reheat cheese in a 300°F oven for a minute or two if it starts to set while serving.

MAKE AHEAD Flatbreads can be stored in an airtight container at room temperature up to 3 days.

HERBED FLATBREAD
makes 16

—

1 teaspoon active dry yeast

1 cup warm water (about 110°F)

3 cups all-purpose flour, plus more for dusting

3 tablespoons extra-virgin olive oil, plus more for bowl

1 teaspoon sugar

Coarse salt

1 large egg whisked with 1 tablespoon water, for egg wash

Flaky sea salt (such as Maldon)

¼ cup mixed fresh rosemary and thyme leaves

1. Stir yeast into warm water in a bowl; let stand until foamy, 5 minutes. Stir in flour, oil, sugar, and 2 teaspoons coarse salt until dough forms. On a floured surface, knead with floured hands until smooth, 2 minutes. Transfer to an oiled bowl; cover with plastic wrap. Let rise in a warm spot until doubled in bulk, 1 hour.

2. Preheat oven to 350°F. Divide dough into 16 pieces; keep covered. Roll out 1 piece at a time to 4 by 10 inches on floured surface; transfer to parchment-lined baking sheets (4 per sheet). Brush with egg wash; sprinkle with sea salt and herbs. Bake until crisp and golden, rotating sheets halfway through, 18 to 22 minutes. Transfer to a wire rack to cool completely.

Small
Plates

Appetizers that double as dinner should have a bit more heft, and that's what you'll find here, along with a few all-inclusive, serve-yourself spreads. Though they're meant to be served on small plates, each dish is definitely big on satisfaction.

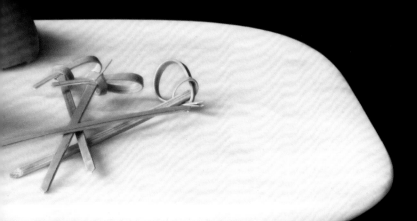

Everybody loves a burger in miniature, but when it comes to serving sliders at a party, don't just stick with beef; instead, offer a variety of options. Here, smoked salmon is mixed into the salmon burgers, and bacon into the turkey burgers; the lamb burgers are topped with a roasted-eggplant relish. Look for miniature brioche buns at bakeries or slider buns at many supermarkets (Pepperidge Farm makes a variety)—or bake your own (see recipe on page 115).

Sliders

BEEF SLIDERS
Makes 20

—

2 pounds ground sirloin

Coarse salt and freshly ground pepper

4 ounces cheddar cheese, thinly sliced, cut into 20 2-inch squares

20 mini hamburger buns (page 115) or brioche buns

Torn lettuce leaves, sliced small plum tomatoes, and dill pickle slices, for serving

1. Form sirloin into 20 patties (each 1 inch thick and 2½ inches in diameter). Place on a rimmed baking sheet. Season with salt and pepper.

2. Heat broiler, with rack about 4 inches from heat source. Broil 4 to 5 minutes for medium-rare. Top each burger with a slice of cheese; broil 30 seconds more.

3. Toast buns. Sandwich each with lettuce, burger, plum tomato slice, and dill pickle slice.

MAKE AHEAD You can form all the patties up to a day ahead; arrange on a parchment-lined baking sheet, cover tightly with plastic wrap, and refrigerate. Let stand at room temperature 30 minutes before cooking.

SERVE ALL WITH

Wings (all variations; pages 122–25)

Summer Crudités with Green Goddess Dip (page 53)

Seasoned Chips (all variations; page 20)

Fried Macaroni-and-Cheese Bites (page 228)

Sliders

GREEK LAMB SLIDERS
makes 20

—

- 3 tablespoons extra-virgin olive oil
- 1 large eggplant (1½ pounds), cut lengthwise into ½-inch-thick strips

  Coarse salt and freshly ground pepper
- 3 tablespoons chopped fresh mint leaves, plus whole leaves for serving

  Finely grated zest of 1 lemon plus 2 teaspoons fresh lemon juice
- 2 pounds ground lamb
- 2½ teaspoons curry powder
- 2½ teaspoons ground coriander
- 20 mini hamburger buns (opposite) or brioche buns

  Feta cheese, crumbled, for serving

1. Heat 2 tablespoons oil in a large skillet over medium-high. Add eggplant and season with salt and pepper. Cook, turning occasionally, until tender and browned, 10 to 12 minutes. Transfer to a cutting board and coarsely chop. In a bowl, toss eggplant with chopped mint and lemon zest and juice.

2. Combine lamb, curry powder, and coriander in a bowl. Mix gently with a fork (do not overmix); form into 20 patties (each 1 inch thick and 2½ inches in diameter). Season with salt and pepper.

3. In a large skillet, heat remaining tablespoon oil over medium-high. Cook patties, flipping once, until browned and just cooked through, about 4 minutes per side (reduce heat if browning too quickly).

4. Toast buns. Sandwich each with burger, eggplant mixture, feta, and whole mint leaves.

SALMON SLIDERS
makes 20

—

- 2 pounds skinless salmon fillets
- 6 ounces thinly sliced smoked salmon, finely chopped
- 3 tablespoons chopped fresh dill
- 1 tablespoon extra-virgin olive oil
- 20 mini hamburger buns (opposite) or brioche buns

  Whole-grain mustard and watercress sprigs, for serving

1. Cut salmon fillets into large chunks. Pulse in a food processor until chopped but not smooth. Transfer to a bowl and mix in smoked salmon and dill. Form into 20 patties (each 1 inch thick and 2½ inches in diameter).

2. Heat oil in a large skillet over medium-high. Cook patties, flipping once, until golden brown and almost cooked through, about 2 minutes per side.

3. Toast buns. Sandwich each with burger, mustard, and watercress.

TURKEY AND AVOCADO SLIDERS
makes 20

▬

2 pounds ground dark-meat turkey (93% lean)

14 bacon slices, finely chopped

Coarse salt

4 ounces Swiss cheese, thinly sliced and cut into 2-inch squares

20 mini hamburger buns (below) or brioche buns

Sliced avocado and mayonnaise, for serving

1. In a bowl, gently mix together ground turkey and bacon. Form into 20 patties (each 1 inch thick and 2½ inches in diameter). Season with salt. Place on a rimmed baking sheet.

2. Heat broiler, with rack 4 inches from heat source. Broil until golden brown and a meat thermometer inserted in centers registers 165°F, 8 to 10 minutes. Top each burger with a slice of cheese; broil 30 seconds more.

3. Toast buns. Sandwich each with burger, sliced avocado, and a dollop of mayonnaise.

Mini Hamburger Buns
makes 50

▬

1 envelope (2¼ teaspoons) active dry yeast

2 tablespoons plus ½ teaspoon sugar

2¼ cups warm water (110°F)

2 large eggs

⅔ cup plus 1 tablespoon powdered milk

2½ teaspoons coarse salt

4½ to 4¾ cups bread flour, plus more for dusting

1 cup (2 sticks) unsalted butter, cut into small pieces, room temperature

Sesame seeds, for sprinkling (optional)

Safflower oil, for coating

1. In a small bowl, sprinkle yeast and ½ teaspoon sugar over ½ cup warm water; stir to combine. Let stand until foamy, about 5 minutes.

2. With an electric mixer on medium-high speed, beat remaining 1¾ cups warm water, 1 egg, powdered milk, 2 tablespoons sugar, salt, and 1 cup flour until smooth and creamy, about 7 minutes.

3. Beat in yeast mixture to combine. With mixer on medium-low speed, beat in 3½ cups flour, ½ cup at a time, until dough comes together (it will be sticky), about 2 minutes. Switch to the dough hook. Gradually add butter; beat until dough is soft and sticks to fingers only slightly, about 7 minutes. If dough is too wet, add ¼ cup more flour.

4. On a lightly floured surface, knead dough several turns into a ball. Coat a large bowl lightly with oil. Add dough, smooth side up. Cover dough with oiled plastic wrap. Let rise in a warm spot until doubled in bulk, about 1 hour.

5. Preheat oven to 350°F. Coat parchment-lined baking sheets lightly with oil. Roll dough into ¾-inch balls; place 1½ inches apart on sheets. Cover with lightly oiled plastic wrap and let rise in a warm spot until doubled in bulk, about 20 minutes.

6. Whisk remaining egg with 1 tablespoon water. Brush egg wash over tops of dough and sprinkle with sesame seeds (if desired). Bake until golden brown, rotating sheets halfway through, 8 to 10 minutes. Transfer sheets to a wire rack and let cool completely.

MAKE AHEAD Baked and cooled buns can be frozen in an airtight container up to 1 week; let thaw at room temperature or reheat (without thawing) in a 300°F oven for about 10 minutes.

When it comes to carefree entertaining, nothing beats an antipasto platter—especially when there's no hard-and-fast meal time, and everything can be served at (or kept at) room temperature. It's simple to procure a nice selection of cured meats, dried sausages, cheeses, and bread, then include a few items you make yourself. Marinated gigante beans and vegetables, as well as cheese-stuffed peppers, can all be put together in advance—and quickly. Wine is a natural drink pairing, but a refreshing Negroni Swizzle (page 236) makes it feel like more of an occasion worth celebrating.

Antipasto

Antipasto

GIGANTE BEANS
serves 8

▬

- ¾ cup dried gigante beans, rinsed (see note, below)
- 2 dried bay leaves
- Coarse salt and freshly ground pepper
- ½ cup extra-virgin olive oil
- 1 small onion, finely chopped
- 1 large carrot, finely chopped
- 1 large celery stalk, finely chopped
- 1 large garlic clove, finely chopped
- ¾ teaspoon aniseeds
- ½ teaspoon red-pepper flakes
- 1½ teaspoons finely grated lemon zest
- 1½ teaspoons fresh thyme leaves
- ½ cup chopped fresh flat-leaf parsley

1. Place beans in a bowl, cover with water, and soak overnight at room temperature.

2. Drain beans and rinse; transfer to a pot, and cover with 6 inches of water. Add bay leaves, and bring to a boil, skimming any foam that rises to the surface. Reduce heat to low, and simmer until beans are tender, 1½ to 2 hours. Season with salt, and cook an additional 5 minutes. Drain beans and discard bay leaves.

3. Meanwhile, heat oil in a large skillet over medium. Add onion, carrot, and celery; season with salt and pepper. Cook, stirring frequently, until vegetables are tender, about 10 minutes. Add garlic, aniseeds, red-pepper flakes, and lemon zest. Cook, stirring, 1 minute. Add beans and thyme and cook, stirring occasionally, 10 minutes. Let cool. Toss with parsley just before serving.

NOTE You'll find gigante beans in Mediterranean stores or at specialty food markets, or substitute Great Northern or cannellini beans.

MARINATED BELL PEPPERS
serves 8

▬

- 4 bell peppers, preferably a mix of red, yellow, and orange
- 2 wide strips lemon zest, plus 2 tablespoons fresh lemon juice
- 2 garlic cloves, smashed
- 3 oregano sprigs
- Coarse salt and freshly ground pepper
- ¼ cup extra-virgin olive oil

1. Roast bell peppers directly over a gas flame, turning with tongs, until charred all over. (Alternatively, roast under the broiler.) Transfer to a bowl, and cover tightly with plastic wrap. Let stand until cool enough to handle, about 10 minutes, then rub off skin with a paper towel. (Do not run peppers under water, or you will wash away the flavor.)

2. Slice peppers in half lengthwise, and remove ribs and seeds. Cut into ½-inch-wide strips and return to bowl. Add lemon zest and juice, garlic, oregano, and oil; season with salt and pepper, and toss to combine. Peppers can be refrigerated, covered, up to 2 days before serving.

PROVOLONE-STUFFED PICKLED CHERRY PEPPERS
makes 20

▬

5 slices prosciutto

4 ounces provolone cheese

20 pickled cherry peppers (from a 32-ounce jar, or see page 61)

Small rosemary sprigs, for garnish

Extra-virgin olive oil, for drizzling

Assorted olives, for serving

Cut each slice of prosciutto into 4 pieces. Cut cheese into ½-inch cubes. Stuff each pepper with prosciutto and cheese. Garnish with rosemary, drizzle with oil, and serve with olives.

MARINATED ARTICHOKE HEARTS
makes 8

▬

1 lemon

2 pounds baby artichokes (about 6), tough outer leaves and stems removed

1 shallot, minced

2 tablespoons Dijon mustard

⅓ cup white-wine vinegar

¾ cup plus 2 tablespoons extra-virgin olive oil

Coarse salt and freshly ground pepper

1. Juice the lemon into a large bowl of water. Halve artichokes; trim any pink choke from the center, leaving artichoke half intact. Trim off ends. Transfer artichokes to lemon water.

2. Drain artichokes, and add to a pot of boiling water. Reduce heat; gently simmer until just tender, 5 to 7 minutes. Transfer to a colander with a slotted spoon.

3. In a bowl, while whisking together shallot, mustard, and vinegar, slowly add oil until emulsified. Season with salt and pepper. Add artichokes, toss to combine, and serve. Artichokes can be refrigerated up to 1 week.

MARINATED ZUCCHINI WITH MINT
Serves 8

▬

6 zucchini, thinly sliced lengthwise

¼ cup extra-virgin olive oil, plus more for drizzling

Coarse salt and freshly ground pepper

2 garlic cloves, minced

2 tablespoons white-wine vinegar

¼ cup fresh mint leaves, torn

1. Preheat oven to 475°F. Divide zucchini among 2 large rimmed baking sheets; drizzle with oil, and season with salt and pepper. Toss to combine, and spread in a single layer. Roast until tender and browned, 10 to 15 minutes.

2. Transfer to a bowl. Sprinkle with garlic, and add oil and vinegar. Let stand 1 hour at room temperature or up to overnight in the refrigerator, covered (bring to room temperature before serving). Sprinkle with mint and serve.

NOTE Any of the following items would make great additions to—or swaps for—the recipes included here.

Melon wedges

Roasted Spiced Chickpeas (page 27)

Eggplant-Caponata Bruschetta (page 135)

Mostardo (candied fruit condiment)

Pepperoncini

Caper berries

Roasted vegetables, such as eggplant, bell peppers, and cauliflower

Gardiniera (pickled carrots, cauliflower, and sweet peppers)

Other good cheeses, such as Taleggio, Pecorino Romano, or fresh mozzarella or bocconcini

There are just a couple of tricks to keep in mind when serving pizza as party food: First, choose a topping that's not too cumbersome, such as the sautéed mushrooms here. Second, shape the dough into long ovals to make it easy to cut the pie into small, slender wedges. If you don't have time to prepare it yourself, from scratch, embrace the convenience of buying dough from your favorite pizzeria or grocer.

Wild Mushroom Pizzas

makes two 6-by-16-inch pies

3 tablespoons unsalted butter

½ cup finely chopped shallots

1½ pounds mixed wild mushrooms, coarsely chopped

Coarse salt and freshly ground pepper

½ cup dry white wine

¾ cup heavy cream

Basic Pizza Dough (recipe page 243)

2 tablespoons extra-virgin olive oil, plus more for drizzling

3 tablespoons fresh tarragon leaves

SERVE WITH

Honey-Roasted Salted Figs (page 39)

Warmed Olives (page 40)

Bacon-Wrapped Blue Cheese–Stuffed Figs (page 72)

Italian Meatballs (page 152)

1. Preheat oven to 500°F, with rack in lowest position and a pizza stone (or inverted rimmed baking sheet) on rack. Melt butter in a large sauté pan over medium-high heat. Add shallots; cook until softened, stirring occasionally, about 2 minutes. Add mushrooms and season with salt and pepper; cook until mushrooms are softened and golden brown, stirring occasionally, about 5 minutes. Add wine, bring to a boil, and cook until evaporated, about 1 minute. Add cream; cook, stirring, until mostly absorbed, about 4 minutes. Transfer to a plate and let cool.

2. Gently stretch each piece of dough (see tip, below) into a 6-by-16-inch oval and place on a piece of parchment. Brush each dough with 1 tablespoon oil, then top with mushroom mixture, dividing evenly and leaving a ½-inch border. Transfer pizzas on parchment onto pizza stone, and bake until crust is golden and crisp, 10 to 12 minutes. Remove from oven. Drizzle with oil, sprinkle with tarragon, and serve, cut into wedges.

TIP To stretch the dough, start by shaping each ball into a round. Hold top edge of dough in both hands, and move hands around edge to form a rough circle, as if turning a wheel. Then begin stretching dough lengthwise into an oval by draping it over the back of your hands and letting its weight pull it into shape, shifting your hands as needed and working from the center to the edges.

Buffalo "hot" wings (pictured below, far left) aren't the only game in town; seasoned chicken wings are popular all over the globe. Just consider the additional options here, all flavored with Asian ingredients—tandoori, ginger-scallion, and miso-honey. We stuck with tradition and fried the all-American original; the rest are baked or broiled. You could even throw a wing party (during football season, or any time of year) featuring all four.

Chicken Wings

Chicken Wings

BUFFALO CHICKEN WINGS
serves 8 to 10

▬

Safflower oil, for frying

3 pounds whole chicken wings (about 32), patted dry

⅔ cup hot sauce, such as Frank's Red Hot

4 tablespoons unsalted butter, melted

Blue Cheese Dipping Sauce, for serving

1. Preheat oven to 225°F. Heat 2 inches oil in a large, deep skillet over medium-high until 375°F on a deep-fry thermometer. Fry chicken in batches until golden brown and cooked through, 10 to 12 minutes. Transfer to a paper-towel-lined baking sheet; keep warm in oven. Return oil to 375°F between batches.

2. In a large bowl, stir together hot sauce and melted butter. Add chicken and toss to coat. Serve wings with dipping sauce.

Blue Cheese Dipping Sauce
makes about 2 cups

▬

1 cup sour cream

2 tablespoons mayonnaise

2 tablespoons milk

1⅓ cups crumbled mild blue cheese

Coarse salt

In a bowl, stir together sour cream, mayonnaise, milk, and blue cheese. Season with salt. Refrigerate, covered, up to 2 days.

SERVE WITH

Seasoned Potato Chips (sea salt and black pepper variation; page 20)

Pigs in Blankets (page 126)

Fried Macaroni-and-Cheese Bites (page 228)

TANDOORI CHICKEN WINGS
serves 8 to 10

▬

½ cup tomato paste

1 tablespoon plus 1 teaspoon garam masala

½ teaspoon ground cinnamon

2 teaspoons ground turmeric

1 teaspoon cayenne pepper

1 tablespoon plus 1 teaspoon grated peeled fresh ginger (from a 2-inch piece)

1 tablespoon plus 1 teaspoon safflower oil, plus more for baking sheets

2 teaspoons coarse salt

3 cups plain Greek yogurt

3 pounds whole chicken wings (about 32), patted dry

1 cup mango chutney

1 tart green apple, such as Granny Smith, grated

1. In a large bowl, combine tomato paste, spices, ginger, oil, salt, and 2 cups yogurt. Slit each chicken wing on the underside, above and below the joints, and add to yogurt mixture. Marinate at least 30 minutes, or up to 8 hours, covered, in the refrigerator (bring to room temperature before cooking).

2. Heat broiler with rack 8 inches from heat source. Lightly oil 2 rimmed baking sheets, and divide wings between sheets in a single layer. Broil each sheet until golden and cooked through, flipping chicken and rotating sheets halfway through, 16 to 18 minutes. Brush wings with chutney. Stir apple into remaining cup yogurt, and serve with wings, for dipping.

SERVE WITH

Red Curry Shrimp Dumplings (page 168)

Papaya, Mango, and Pineapple with Spiced Salt (page 33)

GINGER-SCALLION WINGS
serves 8 to 10

▬

¼ cup safflower oil, plus more for baking sheets

3 pounds whole chicken wings (about 32), patted dry

Coarse salt

8 large scallions, trimmed and sliced

¼ cup finely chopped peeled fresh ginger (from a 4-inch piece)

Toasted sesame seeds, for sprinkling

1. Preheat oven to 450°F. Lightly oil 2 rimmed baking sheets, and divide wings between sheets in a single layer; season with salt. Bake until golden brown and cooked through, flipping chicken and rotating sheets halfway through, about 35 minutes.

2. Meanwhile, in a food processor, process scallions, ginger, 1 teaspoon salt, and oil until smooth. Transfer wings to a large bowl, add scallion paste, and toss to coat. Return wings to sheets, and bake just until set, about 10 minutes. Sprinkle with sesame seeds and serve.

─────────

SERVE WITH

Seasoned Chips (Japanese rice powder variation; page 20)

Summer Rolls (any variation; pages 162–165)

Pork and Chive Pot Stickers (page 166)

MISO-HONEY WINGS
serves 8 to 10

▬

Safflower oil

3 pounds whole chicken wings (about 32), patted dry

Coarse salt and freshly ground pepper

⅔ cup honey

⅓ cup white or yellow miso

1. Preheat oven to 450°F. Lightly oil 2 rimmed baking sheets, and divide wings between sheets in a single layer; season with salt and pepper. Bake until golden brown and cooked through, flipping chicken and rotating sheets halfway through, about 35 minutes.

2. Combine honey and miso in a small bowl, and season with pepper. Brush wings with glaze; bake 3 minutes more. Remove from oven, brush with more glaze, and serve.

─────────

SERVE WITH

Chinese Five-Spice Pecans (page 19)

Summer Rolls (any variation; pages 162–165)

Red Curry Shrimp Dumplings (page 168)

─────────

TIP Buy whole wings, with the tips intact. Besides making a better presentation, the tips give you something to hold onto while eating the wings, and they turn wonderfully crunchy in the oven (for the last bite).

Try on pigs in blankets for size the next time you're looking for a top-notch, somewhat surprising hit at a cocktail party. Inevitably they're the first thing to run out. Ours have a layer of honey mustard inside and a sprinkling of poppy seeds or flaky sea salt on top. And here's a neat shortcut: Instead of forming individual appetizers, we wrapped four-inch pastry squares (cut from a larger square) around five-inch-long sausages, then sliced them into bite-size pieces. You can even do this ahead (see note, below).

Pigs in Blankets

—

makes 54

All-purpose flour, for dusting

2 sheets puff pastry, preferably all-butter (see note, page 57)

Honey Dijon mustard, for brushing (store-bought or see page 149)

18 fully cooked sausages (each about 5 inches long), such as frankfurters, andouille, or chicken sausages

1 large egg, lightly beaten

Poppy seeds, for sprinkling

Flaky sea salt, such as Maldon, for sprinkling

Assorted mustards, such as yellow, brown, and whole-grain, for serving

1. On a lightly floured work surface, roll out each pastry sheet into a 12-inch square. Trim edges to make even, then cut into 4-inch squares. Lightly brush lower half of each square with honey Dijon mustard, center a sausage on mustard-coated edge, and brush top inch with egg. Roll sausages in pastry, pressing seams to tightly seal. Brush tops with egg, then sprinkle with poppy seeds or flaky salt. Cut each on the bias into thirds. Freeze pigs in blankets, uncovered, on a parchment-lined rimmed baking sheet until firm, at least 1 hour.

2. Preheat oven to 400°F. Place frozen pigs in blankets 1 inch apart on parchment-lined rimmed baking sheets. Bake until pastry is puffed and golden brown, rotating sheets halfway through, about 25 minutes. Serve hot, with mustards.

MAKE AHEAD Once pigs in blankets are frozen until firm, transfer to resealable plastic bags and freeze up to 1 month. Bake straight from freezer as directed.

SERVE WITH

Spiced Cream-Cheese Dips (page 24)

Hot Artichoke Dip (page 68)

Buffalo Chicken Wings (page 124)

No tapas party would be complete without tortilla Española, the national dish of Spain. But this baked omelet fits into all kinds of menus. Our summery version includes thinly sliced zucchini and basil along with the traditional potato. It's dolloped with romesco sauce, another Spanish specialty made from piquillo peppers, almonds, sherry vinegar, and garlic, and is one of our favorite condiments; try it also as a topping for toasts or grilled clams, or as a dip.

Tortilla Española

serves 10 to 12

1 pound zucchini (about 2 medium), sliced into ⅛-inch-thick rounds

2 teaspoons coarse salt

1¼ cups extra-virgin olive oil

2 pounds Yukon Gold potatoes (about 6), scrubbed and sliced ⅛ inch thick

1 large Spanish onion, sliced ⅛ inch thick

10 large eggs

1 cup finely grated Parmigiano-Reggiano cheese

1 cup fresh basil leaves, chopped

Romesco Sauce (page 244), for serving

SERVE WITH

Roasted Spiced Chickpeas (page 27)

Roasted Cauliflower and Manchego Hand Pies (page 160)

Pan Tomate (page 231)

1. In a colander set over a bowl, toss zucchini with salt. Let drain 30 minutes, pressing on zucchini a few times to remove excess moisture.

2. Meanwhile, heat 1 cup oil in a 12-inch ovenproof skillet (preferably cast-iron) over high. Add potatoes and onion; reduce heat to low. Cook, stirring occasionally and scraping up browned bits from bottom of pan, until potatoes are tender but not taking on any color, 30 to 35 minutes.

3. Add zucchini; cook, stirring occasionally, until tender, 12 to 15 minutes. Transfer mixture to colander; let drain 5 minutes, gently stirring occasionally. In a large bowl, whisk together eggs, cheese, and basil; stir in potato mixture.

4. Preheat oven to 425°F. Wipe skillet clean, making sure to remove any browned bits. Heat remaining ¼ cup oil in skillet over high until shimmering. Add egg mixture, and reduce heat to low. Cook, running a flexible spatula around sides occasionally to prevent eggs from sticking, until edges begin to set, about 10 minutes.

5. Transfer to oven. Bake until center is set and edges are golden brown, about 12 minutes. Let cool 5 minutes. Run a knife around edges to loosen, then invert onto a wire rack. Using a large spatula, flip tortilla back over; let cool completely. To serve, cut tortilla into wedges and top with romesco.

MAKE AHEAD The tortilla can be refrigerated, covered, up to 2 days; let cool completely before storing.

You don't have to live on the coast to make lobster rolls from scratch. Lobster is shipped to markets all over the country, and you can even buy it shelled and cooked—although boiling lobster takes no time and, with the right tools, the meat is easy to extract (see notes, below). Buttery pull-apart rolls are the right size for holding the sandwich in one hand and a drink in the other, and they make a fun display.

Pull-Apart Lobster Rolls

makes 12

1   pound cooked lobster meat (from 3 lob-sters; see notes, right), chopped (2¼ cups)

½   cup mayonnaise

2   tablespoons fresh lemon juice

2   tablespoons minced fresh chives

1   tablespoon fresh chervil, plus more for serving

1   teaspoon coarse salt

¼   teaspoon Old Bay seasoning

⅛   teaspoon cayenne pepper

12   pull-apart rolls, such as King's Hawaiian sweet dinner rolls or Martin's potato rolls (do not separate rolls)

4   tablespoons unsalted butter, melted

1. Preheat oven to 350°F. Gently stir to combine lobster, mayonnaise, lemon juice, chives, chervil, salt, Old Bay, and cayenne in a bowl.

2. Split buns across top; brush generously with some of melted butter. Heat on a baking sheet until warmed through, 3 to 5 minutes. Divide lobster salad evenly among rolls, drizzle with remaining butter, sprinkle with chervil, and serve.

SERVE WITH

Seasoned Potato Chips (any variation; page 20)

Bacon-Wrapped Potatoes (page 72)

Classic Deviled Eggs (page 180)

Notes

HOW TO COOK LIVE LOBSTERS
Fill a large stockpot three quarters of the way with cold water; bring to a rolling boil and add a generous amount of coarse salt. Plunge 3 lobsters, one at a time, headfirst into the water, and cook (uncovered) until they turn bright red, 8 to 14 minutes. Use tongs to remove them from the pot, and transfer to a platter. When cool enough to handle, snip tips off claws and let liquid drain out. Remove rubber bands.

HOW TO EXTRACT THE MEAT
Pull claws from bodies, completely separating. Twist each tail from joint where it meets the body. Use kitchen shears to slice down centers of tails. Open sides of tails apart to release the meat. Use your fingers to pull meat from tails. Separate knuckles from claws. Crack knuckles open, and remove meat with a small fork. Grasp "thumbs" from claws, and bend back to snap off. Place claws on their sides on a work surface. Holding with one hand, and using back (dull edge) of a chef's knife, whack several times to crack shells without cutting into meat. Twist to open and then pull out the meat with your fingers. Cut all meat into ½-inch pieces and chop.

Toast or grill thick slices of rustic bread, then rub with halved garlic cloves, drizzle with extra-virgin olive oil, and sprinkle with salt—that's what makes bruschetta a first-rate base for a range of toppings. Thanks to protein-rich items such as beans and tuna, along with cheese and hearty vegetables, each of the options here is nothing short of satisfying, and can double as dinner.

Bruschetta with Assorted Toppings

BRUSCHETTA
makes about 20

▬

- 1 loaf rustic Italian bread or baguette
- 4 garlic cloves, halved

    Extra-virgin olive oil, for drizzling

    Coarse salt

    Toppings (recipes follow)

Heat broiler with rack 4 inches from heat source. Cut bread into ½-inch-thick slices on the bias. Arrange in a single layer on a rimmed baking sheet. Broil until toasted and crisp, 1 to 2 minutes. Rub with the cut sides of garlic halves, then drizzle with oil and sprinkle with salt.

MAKE AHEAD Toasts can be stored in an airtight container at room temperature up to 1 day.

CHICKPEA, OLIVE, AND TUNA
makes 20

▬

- 3 tablespoons extra-virgin olive oil, plus more for drizzling
- 2 garlic cloves, thinly sliced
- 2 cans (each 15.5 ounces) chickpeas, drained and rinsed

    Crushed red-pepper flakes

- 1 cup pitted Kalamata olives, halved

    Coarse salt and freshly ground black pepper

    Bruschetta

- 1 jar (6.7 ounces) oil-packed tuna, preferably fillets, flaked into bite-size pieces

1. Heat oil in a large skillet over medium-high. Add garlic and cook, stirring, just until fragrant. Add chickpeas and season with red-pepper flakes; cook, tossing, until warmed through, about 5 minutes. Stir in olives. Season with salt. Lightly mash mixture with a fork.

2. Dividing evenly, spoon chickpea mixture on toasts and drizzle with more oil; top with tuna, season with black pepper, and serve.

Assorted Toppings for Bruschetta

BROCCOLI RABE AND RICOTTA SALATA
makes 20

- 1 bunch broccoli rabe (about 1 pound), trimmed and cut into 1½-inch pieces
- 1 garlic clove, minced
- ¼ teaspoon red-pepper flakes, plus more for serving
- Extra-virgin olive oil, for drizzling
- Coarse salt
- Juice of 1 lemon
- Bruschetta (page 133)
- 4 ounces ricotta salata, shaved

1. Preheat oven to 450°F. Combine broccoli rabe, garlic, and red-pepper flakes on a rimmed baking sheet; drizzle with olive oil, and season with salt. Toss by hand, massaging oil into greens. Spread in a single layer. Roast until tender, about 15 minutes.

2. Dividing evenly, spoon mixture on toasts; drizzle with lemon juice and more oil, top with shaved cheese and more red-pepper flakes, and serve.

ROASTED TOMATOES AND AGED GOAT CHEESE
makes 20

- 2 pints cherry or grape tomatoes, preferably a mixture of yellow, orange, and red
- Extra-virgin olive oil, for drizzling
- Coarse salt and freshly ground pepper
- 8 ounces aged goat cheese, such as Humboldt Fog, thinly sliced
- Bruschetta (page 133)

1. Preheat oven to 500°F. Spread tomatoes in a single layer on a rimmed baking sheet. Drizzle with oil, and season with salt and pepper. Roast until just starting to burst, about 10 minutes.

2. Dividing evenly, top toasts with cheese and then tomatoes; drizzle with juices from baking sheet and serve.

SERVE ALL WITH

Italian Meatballs (page 152)

Bacon-Wrapped Blue Cheese–Stuffed Figs (page 72)

Warmed Olives (page 40)

Prosciutto-Wrapped Asparagus (page 38)

EGGPLANT CAPONATA
makes 20

—

2 tablespoons extra-virgin olive oil

1 large onion, finely chopped

2 garlic cloves, thinly sliced

2 tablespoons golden raisins

2 tablespoons pine nuts

¼ to ½ teaspoon red-pepper flakes

½ cup tomato paste

2 tablespoons sugar

1 small eggplant, coarsely chopped

⅓ cup white-wine vinegar

Coarse salt

Bruschetta (page 133)

1. In a Dutch oven or heavy pot, heat oil over medium-high. Add onion, garlic, raisins, pine nuts, and red-pepper flakes (to taste). Cook, stirring occasionally, until onion is softened, 2 to 3 minutes.

2. Add tomato paste and sugar; cook, stirring, until fragrant, 2 to 3 minutes. Add eggplant, vinegar, and ⅓ cup water. Cover and cook, stirring occasionally, until eggplant is tender and mixture is thick, about 10 minutes. Season with coarse salt.

3. Dividing evenly, spoon eggplant mixture on toasts, and serve.

MAKE AHEAD Caponata can be refrigerated in an airtight container up to 5 days; let cool before storing and reheat over low before serving.

MASHED WHITE BEANS AND SAGE
makes 20

—

2 cans (each 15.5 ounces) cannellini beans, drained and rinsed

2 garlic cloves

2 tablespoons extra-virgin olive oil

4 fresh sage leaves, minced, plus whole leaves for garnish

Juice of 1 lemon

Coarse salt and freshly ground pepper

2 tablespoons safflower oil, for frying (optional)

Bruschetta (page 133)

1. Mash beans with a fork in a bowl. Add garlic, olive oil, sage, and lemon juice, and mix to combine. Season with salt and pepper.

2. For garnish (if desired), heat safflower oil over medium-high in a skillet until shimmering. Fry whole sage leaves until crisp, 1 to 2 minutes. Use a slotted spoon to transfer to paper towels to drain.

3. Dividing evenly, spoon bean mixture on toasts; garnish with fried sage leaves, and serve.

Tender crust surrounding a savory, delicious filling—that about sums up empanadas' appeal. That they come in portable packages helps, too. Spicy pork is among the most traditional, but you'll find countless other fillings that are just as tasty, like roasted shallots and dates; chicken with chipotle, pepitas, and cilantro; and beef with olives and raisins (the classic). If you make more than one type at once, mark each variety with its own seal—crimp with a fork, cut slits with a knife, or pinch with the tip of a small spoon—to distinguish it from the others. See page 138 for make-ahead information.

Mini Empanadas

PORK EMPANADAS
makes 48

For the filling

- 1 pound ground pork
- 1 onion, finely diced
- 1 jalapeño chile, minced (ribs and seeds removed for less heat, if desired)
- ¼ teaspoon ground dried chile
- 1 can (14.5 ounces) diced tomatoes
- Coarse salt and freshly ground pepper
- ½ cup fresh cilantro leaves, coarsely chopped

For the dough

- 6 cups all-purpose flour, plus more for dusting
- 1 tablespoon baking powder
- 1 tablespoon coarse salt
- ¾ cup (1½ sticks) cold unsalted butter, cut into small pieces
- 2 large eggs whisked with 2 tablespoons water, for egg wash

1. Make the filling: In a 12-inch skillet, cook pork over medium-high heat, breaking it up with a spoon, until browned, 5 to 7 minutes. Add onion and jalapeño; cook, stirring occasionally, until soft, about 5 minutes. Stir in ground chile and tomatoes. Cook over medium heat, stirring occasionally, until mixture has thickened, 12 to 15 minutes. Season with salt and pepper. Stir in cilantro. Let cool completely.

2. Meanwhile, make the dough: Combine flour, baking powder, and salt in a bowl. Using your fingers, work in butter until mixture is crumbly. Add just enough cold water (about 1½ cups) so dough comes together. Turn out onto a lightly floured surface, and knead to form a smooth ball. Cut ball into 4 equal pieces. Cover with plastic wrap; let stand 20 minutes.

3. Break off a 1½-inch ball of dough. On a clean work surface, roll dough out into a circle, about ⅛ inch thick. Using a 3-inch cookie cutter (or an inverted glass and a paring knife), cut out a round of dough. Place 1 tablespoon filling in center of round. Using a pastry brush, moisten edges of dough with water; fold dough over to seal, pressing gently. Crimp edges with a fork. Repeat with remaining dough and filling. Gather dough scraps, and reroll once to cut out more rounds.

4. Preheat oven to 400°F. Place empanadas on a parchment-lined baking sheet. Brush egg wash over tops, avoiding crimped edges. Bake until golden brown, rotating sheets halfway through, 30 to 40 minutes. Let cool slightly before serving.

Fillings for Mini Empanadas

SPICY CHICKEN WITH THYME
makes 48

—

1 bone-in, skin-on chicken breast (about 1 pound)

1 white onion, cut into 4 wedges, 2 wedges finely chopped

1 dried bay leaf

2 teaspoons extra-virgin olive oil

2 garlic cloves, minced

¾ teaspoon ground cumin

¼ teaspoon ground cinnamon (preferably Mexican canela)

4 canned whole peeled tomatoes, chopped

2 canned chipotle chiles in adobo, chopped

1 poblano chile, roasted (see page 242) and cut into ¼-inch strips

Coarse salt and freshly ground pepper

2 tablespoons coarsely chopped fresh cilantro leaves

1 tablespoon toasted pepitas (see page 242), coarsely chopped

Dough for empanadas (page 137)

4 ounces queso blanco or feta cheese, crumbled

1. In a large saucepan, combine chicken, onion wedges, and bay leaf with enough cold water to cover. Bring to a boil, then reduce heat and simmer until chicken is cooked through, about 15 minutes. Transfer to a plate; reserve 1 cup cooking liquid and discard onion and bay leaf. When chicken is cool enough to handle, shred meat into bite-size pieces (discard skin and bones).

2. Heat oil in a medium saucepan over medium. Add chopped onion and garlic. Cook, stirring occasionally, until soft, 2 to 3 minutes. Add cumin and cinnamon; cook, stirring, until fragrant, about 30 seconds. Add tomatoes, chipotle chiles, poblano chile, shredded chicken, and reserved cooking liquid. Cook over medium-low heat, stirring occasionally, until liquid has thickened, about 25 minutes. Remove from heat. Season with salt and pepper. Stir in cilantro and pepitas. Let cool completely.

3. Follow recipe to make the dough and cut into rounds. Place 1 tablespoon chicken mixture in center of each round; top with 1 teaspoon cheese. Form into half-moons, and bake as directed.

MAKE AHEAD Empanadas can be filled and formed (omit egg wash), then frozen in a single layer on a baking sheet until firm, about 2 hours; transfer to resealable plastic bags, and freeze up to 3 months. When ready to bake, arrange on baking sheet and brush with egg wash (no need to thaw); bake 2 to 3 minutes longer than suggested in recipe.

ROASTED SHALLOT AND DATE
makes 48

—

2 pounds small shallots (about 32),
  root ends trimmed (do not peel)

2 tablespoons unsalted butter, melted

1 tablespoon sugar

  Coarse salt and freshly ground pepper

  Dough for empanadas (page 137): add
  $2\frac{1}{4}$ teaspoons crushed caraway seeds to
  the flour mixture before working in butter

12 dried dates, pitted and quartered

1 tablespoon plus 1 teaspoon fresh thyme
  leaves

1. Preheat oven to 350°F. Combine shallots, butter, and sugar in a baking pan just large enough to hold shallots in a single layer; season with salt and pepper, and toss to combine. Cover with parchment, then foil; bake, stirring every 20 minutes, until shallots are very tender and caramelized, $1\frac{1}{2}$ to $1\frac{3}{4}$ hours. When cool enough to handle, remove skins; slice shallots into thirds.

2. Follow recipe to make the dough (adding caraway seeds) and cut into rounds. Place 2 date quarters in center of each round, then top with 1 tablespoon shallot mixture. Add a pinch of thyme; season with salt and pepper. Form into half-moons, and bake as directed.

BEEF EMPANADAS WITH OLIVES AND RAISINS
makes 48

—

1 tablespoon extra-virgin olive oil

1 small onion, finely chopped

1 small green bell pepper, finely chopped

1 pound ground beef

1 teaspoon ground cumin

$\frac{3}{4}$ cup pimiento-filled green olives, sliced

$\frac{3}{4}$ cup raisins

  Coarse salt and freshly ground pepper

  Dough for empanadas (page 137)

1. Heat oil in a large skillet over medium-high. Add onion and bell pepper. Cook until softened, about 3 minutes. Add beef and cook, stirring frequently, until no longer pink, 5 to 7 minutes. Add cumin; cook, stirring, 1 minute.

2. Stir in olives and raisins; season with salt and pepper. Cook until meat is browned and liquid has evaporated, about 5 minutes.

3. Follow recipe to make the dough and cut into rounds. Place 1 tablespoon filling in center of each round. Form into half-moons, and bake as directed.

SERVE ALL WITH

Guacamole (any variation;
pages 64–65)

Salsas (any variation;
page 31)

**Papaya, Mango, and
Pineapple with Spiced Salt**
(page 33)

A little of this, a little of that—a traditional mezze (here, with a few twists) is a wise idea for any host. Most of the components—including hummus and other spreads and even dolmades (stuffed grape leaves)—can and should be made ahead, allowing their flavors time to meld. And while ouzo would be more than fine on its own, here it is mixed with lemon-flavored simple syrup for a zesty cocktail.

Mezze

Mezze

TABBOULEH
makes 4 cups

—

½ cup bulgur

4 plum tomatoes, seeds removed, finely chopped (juices reserved)

1¾ cups finely chopped fresh flat-leaf parsley leaves

4 scallions, trimmed and finely chopped

¼ cup fresh lemon juice (from 2 lemons)

¼ cup extra-virgin olive oil

Coarse salt and freshly ground pepper

2 tablespoons finely chopped mint leaves

1. In a bowl, soak bulgur in cold water to cover for 10 minutes to plump the grains; drain.

2. In a large bowl, stir to combine bulgur, tomatoes and their juices, parsley, and scallions. Add lemon juice and oil, and season with salt and pepper. Toss to coat. Tabbouleh can be refrigerated, covered, up to 3 days.

3. Before serving, bring to room temperature and stir in mint.

SPICE-RUBBED PITA CRISPS
makes 12

—

6 pita breads (6 or 8 inch)

Extra-virgin olive oil, for brushing

Za'atar spice blend, for sprinkling

Preheat oven to 400°F. Slit open pitas. Brush split sides generously with oil and sprinkle evenly with za'atar. Place in a single layer on rimmed baking sheets. Bake until crisp and just golden, about 10 minutes. Pitas can be stored in an airtight container, between parchment, at room temperature up to 1 day.

MUHAMMARA
makes 2¼ cups

—

1 pita bread (6 inch), plus more for serving

1 garlic clove

¼ cup walnuts, toasted (see page 242)

1½ teaspoons paprika, plus more for serving

¾ teaspoon ground cumin

3 roasted red bell peppers (see page 242), chopped

1 tablespoon pomegranate molasses

1 tablespoon fresh lemon juice

2 teaspoons extra-virgin olive oil, plus more for drizzling

Coarse salt and freshly ground pepper

1. Preheat oven to 350°F. Toast pita on a baking sheet until crisp and golden, 7 to 8 minutes. Break into 2-inch pieces; place in a bowl, and cover with 1 cup water. Soak until soft, about 10 minutes. Drain in a sieve, pressing out excess water.

2. In a food processor, pulse garlic and walnuts until finely chopped. Add paprika, cumin, bell peppers, and pita; process until smooth. Add pomegranate molasses, lemon juice, and oil; season with salt and pepper. Pulse until combined. Transfer to a bowl; cover and refrigerate at least 1 hour or up to 1 day.

3. Before serving, bring to room temperature, drizzle with oil, and sprinkle with paprika. Serve with pita.

EGGPLANT CAPONATA (see page 135 for recipe; omit step 3)

HUMMUS
makes 3 cups

▬

2 cans (15.5 ounces each) chickpeas, drained and rinsed

⅓ cup fresh lemon juice (from 2 lemons)

¼ cup tahini (well stirred)

⅓ cup extra-virgin olive oil, plus more for drizzling

1 garlic clove, smashed

⅛ teaspoon cayenne pepper

Coarse salt and freshly ground black pepper

Sumac or aleppo pepper, lightly toasted pine nuts (see page 242), and fresh mint and/or flat-leaf parsley leaves, for serving

1. In a food processor, combine chickpeas, lemon juice, tahini, oil, garlic, and cayenne; season with salt. Process until combined but not completely smooth, then transfer to a bowl. Hummus can be refrigerated, covered, up to 2 days.

2. Before serving, bring to room temperature; drizzle with more oil, sprinkle with sumac or aleppo pepper, and top with pine nuts and herbs.

STUFFED GRAPE LEAVES (DOLMADES)
makes 35

▬

½ onion, minced

¼ cup plus 2 tablespoons uncooked white rice

1 pound ground lamb

1 small garlic clove, minced

3 tablespoons finely chopped fresh flat-leaf parsley leaves

1 small carrot, peeled and finely chopped

1 teaspoon finely grated lemon zest

1 heaping tablespoon fresh mint leaves, chopped, plus 3 sprigs

½ tablespoon coarse salt

¼ teaspoon freshly ground pepper

¼ cup extra-virgin olive oil, plus more for drizzling

1 jar (16 ounces) grape leaves, drained and rinsed

3 cups low-sodium chicken broth

1 lemon, halved, one half sliced into rounds

1. Preheat oven to 325°F. In a bowl, mix onion, rice, lamb, garlic, parsley, carrot, lemon zest, chopped mint, salt, pepper, and 1 tablespoon oil. Place 1 grape leaf, vein side up, on a work surface. Place 1 tablespoon filling just below center. Fold bottom of leaf over filling, and fold in sides; roll up. Do not overfill. Repeat with remaining leaves and filling.

2. Lay stuffed leaves, seam sides down, in a 9-by-13-inch nonreactive baking dish. Combine broth and remaining 3 tablespoons oil; pour over dolmades. Squeeze lemon half over dolmades, and top with lemon slices and mint sprigs. Weight with another 9-by-13-inch baking dish filled halfway with water.

3. Bake 40 to 50 minutes. Remove from oven; let dolmades cool in cooking liquid, still weighted, for 2 hours. Serve at room temperature, drizzled with more oil.

MAKE AHEAD Cooked dolmades can be refrigerated up to 2 days; bring to room temperature before drizzling with olive oil and serving.

It's easy to overlook quesadillas (kids' favorites) as party food for grownups. Yet the basic formula—tortillas layered with cheese and other fillings—is open to endless interpretations (especially for vegetarian options). Take the ones here, which incorporate corn, roasted chile peppers, black beans, chicken, and sweet potatoes. It's fun to make all three, and serve with sour cream, salsa, and pickled jalapeños alongside.

Quesadillas

SWEET POTATO AND POBLANO
makes 5

- 2 sweet potatoes, scrubbed
- 10 flour tortillas (8 inch)
- 3 poblano chiles, roasted (see page 242) and cut into thin strips
- 2½ cups shredded Monterey Jack cheese
  Coarse salt and freshly ground pepper

1. Preheat oven to 400°F. Prick sweet potatoes with a fork. Bake on a baking sheet until tender, about 1 hour. Remove from oven; when cool enough to handle, scoop out flesh and mash. Season with salt and pepper.

2. Dividing evenly, spread sweet-potato mixture over 5 tortillas, then top with chiles and cheese. Top evenly with remaining tortillas, pressing gently.

3. Heat a large cast-iron skillet over medium. Cook each quesadilla until golden brown and cheese is melting, 2 to 3 minutes per side. Serve immediately with accompaniments.

CHORIZO, CORN, AND CHEDDAR
makes 5

- 10 flour tortillas (8 inch)
- 2½ cups shredded cheddar cheese
- 12 ounces cooked chorizo, coarsely chopped
- 1⅔ cups fresh (from 3 ears) or thawed frozen corn kernels

1. Dividing evenly, top 5 tortillas with cheese, chorizo, and corn. Top with remaining tortillas, pressing gently.

2. Heat a large cast-iron skillet over medium. Cook each quesadilla until golden brown and cheese is melting, 2 to 3 minutes per side. Serve immediately with accompaniments.

CHICKEN, BLACK BEAN, AND GOAT CHEESE
makes 5

- ½ cup plus 2 tablespoons fresh goat cheese
- ½ cup plus 2 tablespoons sour cream
- 10 flour tortillas (8 inch)
- 1¼ cups canned black beans, drained and rinsed
- 1 cooked bone-in, skin-on chicken breast half (8 ounces), shredded (see step 1 of recipe on page 138)
- 1 bunch scallions, trimmed and thinly sliced

1. Stir together goat cheese and sour cream in a bowl. Dividing evenly, spread goat-cheese mixture over 5 tortillas, then top with black beans, chicken, and scallions. Top with remaining tortillas, pressing gently.

2. Heat a large cast-iron skillet over medium. Cook each quesadilla until golden brown and cheese is melting, 2 to 3 minutes per side. Serve immediately with accompaniments.

SERVE ALL WITH

Classic Guacamole (page 64)

Salsas (any variation; page 31)

Mini Chicken Flautas (page 95)

Yellow-Tomato and Mango Gazpacho (page 218)

Here's a party trick that the most experienced hosts have long known: Instead of making and assembling a group of different appetizers, offer one big ham and dozens of miniature biscuits, then let your guests build their own bites. Homemade honey mustard and store-bought jams and jellies—lingonberry is shown here, but other flavors such as fig, apricot, or hot pepper would also be good—round out this open-house do-it-yourself spread. The ham serves a sizable crowd, so you may want to bake extra batches of biscuits (see make ahead information on page 149).

Ham and Biscuits

Ham and Biscuits

GLAZED HAM
serves 30 to 40

—

- 1 smoked ham (10 to 14 pounds), bone in and rind on (see note, opposite)
- ½ cup honey
- ¼ teaspoon ground allspice
- ⅓ cup lightly packed grated fresh horseradish (from a 6-inch piece of peeled horseradish root) or ¼ cup prepared horseradish
- Coarse salt and freshly ground pepper
- Angel Biscuits (recipe follows)
- Chive and Black Pepper Biscuits (opposite)
- Honey Mustard (opposite) and jam, for serving

1. Preheat oven to 350°F with rack in lower third. Rinse and dry ham; wrap in parchment, then in foil, making sure thicker rind faces up. Place on a wire rack set in a rimmed baking sheet or roasting pan, and bake 1½ hours.

2. Meanwhile, in a small bowl, stir together honey, allspice, horseradish, ½ teaspoon salt, and ½ teaspoon pepper.

3. Remove ham from oven and unwrap. When cool enough to handle, peel rind from ham with a paring knife, trimming fat to about ½ inch. Pat dry. Score skin with a ¼-inch-deep diamond pattern, spacing lines 1 inch apart.

4. Bake 30 minutes. Baste with honey-horseradish mixture, and continue to bake, basting every 30 minutes, until a thermometer inserted into thickest part of flesh near (but not touching) bone registers 145°F, about 2 hours more. If necessary, add water to pan, about ¼ cup at a time, to prevent pan from scorching, and tent with foil if ham begins to blacken. Transfer to a serving platter; let rest at least 20 minutes before carving. Serve warm or at room temperature, with biscuits, honey mustard, and jam.

ANGEL BISCUITS
makes 48

- 2 envelopes (2¼ teaspoons each) active dry yeast
- ¼ cup warm water (110°F)
- 5 cups all-purpose flour, plus more for dusting
- 1 tablespoon baking powder
- 1 teaspoon baking soda
- 2 tablespoons plus 1½ teaspoons sugar
- 1 teaspoon coarse salt
- 1 cup (2 sticks) cold unsalted butter, cut into small pieces, plus 4 tablespoons, melted and cooled, for brushing
- 2 cups buttermilk

1. Preheat oven to 450°F with racks in upper and lower thirds. Stir yeast into the warm water; let stand until foamy, 5 minutes.

2. Whisk together flour, baking powder, baking soda, sugar, and salt in a large bowl. Transfer half of flour mixture to a food processor; add cold butter, and pulse until mixture resembles coarse meal, with some larger pieces of butter still remaining. Return to bowl; mix to combine with remaining flour mixture. Make a well in the center; add yeast mixture and buttermilk. Stir with a fork just until a dough forms.

3. Turn out onto a floured surface, and knead until smooth and no longer sticky, about 5 minutes. Roll out dough ½ inch thick. Cut out rounds with a floured 1½-inch biscuit cutter. Gather scraps and reroll dough once to cut out more biscuits.

4. Place 1 inch apart on parchment-lined baking sheets, and brush tops with melted butter. Bake until lightly golden (they should not brown), rotating sheets halfway through, 10 to 12 minutes. Serve warm or at room temperature.

CHIVE AND BLACK PEPPER BISCUITS
makes 48

▬

4 cups all-purpose flour, plus more
for dusting

3 tablespoons snipped fresh chives

1 tablespoon baking powder

½ teaspoon baking soda

1 teaspoon coarse salt

2 teaspoons freshly ground pepper

1 cup (2 sticks) cold unsalted butter,
cut into small pieces

1½ cups buttermilk

1. Preheat oven to 425°F with racks in upper
and lower thirds. Whisk together flour,
chives, baking powder, baking soda, salt, and
pepper in a bowl. Cut in butter with a pastry
cutter or your fingers until mixture resembles
coarse crumbs, with larger pieces of butter
remaining. Stir in buttermilk. Dough should
be slightly sticky; do not overmix.

2. Turn out dough onto a lightly floured
surface, and pat into a ¾-inch-thick round
using floured fingers; do not overwork dough.
Cut out rounds with a floured 1½-inch biscuit
cutter. Gather scraps and reroll dough once to
cut out more biscuits.

3. Place 1 inch apart on parchment-lined
baking sheets. Bake until puffed and
golden, rotating sheets halfway through,
14 to 16 minutes. Serve warm or at room
temperature.

Honey Mustard
makes about 1 cup

▬

¼ cup honey

¾ cup Dijon mustard

In a small bowl, stir together honey
and mustard.

NOTE

For the uninitiated, buying a
smoked ham can be a bit intimi-
dating, so it helps to know what
you are looking for. A whole ham
is the entire hind leg of a hog,
which can weigh upward of
15 pounds.

Far more common are half hams;
look for those that are from the
shank end, or the part of the
leg closest to the trotter. The
shank has less connective tissue
and fat than the butt end, cooks
more evenly, makes for a more
striking presentation, and is
easier to carve.

Hams are cured by various
methods, too: a "country" ham is
dry and salty, while a so-called
city-cured ham, like the one
shown on page 146, is more
tender and succulent. It may
be labeled "partially cooked,"
but the way you prepare it is the
same.

MAKE AHEAD Prepare biscuit
doughs and cut into rounds, then
place close, but not touching, on
parchment-lined baking sheets.
Cover with plastic wrap, and
freeze until firm, about 1 hour;
then transfer to a resealable
plastic bag, and freeze up to
1 month. Bake (as many as you
need) as directed, without
thawing, for about 5 minutes
longer than the suggested time.
You can also freeze baked and
cooled biscuits in an airtight
container up to 1 week; thaw
at room temperature or reheat
straight from the freezer in a
300°F oven for about 5 minutes.

It's much easier to make one big tart and cut it into single-serving pieces than to make a bunch of tartlets. Opt for just one tart (such as the Provençal Onion Tart on page 80, or any one of the combinations below) or mix it up—as in this puzzle-piece rearrangement of three versions: potato and rosemary; asparagus and Gruyère; and harissa, goat cheese, and fresh herbs. The blank canvas of puff pastry sparks the imagination.

Puff Pastry Tarts

HARISSA AND GOAT CHEESE PUFF
serves 4

—

- 1 sheet frozen puff pastry, preferably all-butter (see note page 57), thawed

  All-purpose flour, for dusting

- 2 tablespoons harissa
- 2 tablespoons extra-virgin olive oil
- 4 ounces fresh goat cheese, crumbled

  Flaky sea salt, such as Maldon, for serving

  Small fresh mint and flat-leaf parsley leaves, for serving

1. Preheat oven to 400°F. Lay pastry sheet on a lightly floured surface, and roll out into a 10-by-16-inch rectangle. Trim edges with a sharp knife. Transfer to a parchment-lined baking sheet. Use knife to score a 1-inch border around pastry (do not cut all the way through), then pierce inside the markings at ½-inch intervals with a fork.

2. In a small bowl, mix harissa and oil; spread inside border.

3. Bake until crust is golden, about 15 minutes. Top with goat cheese, and bake 5 minutes more. Serve warm, sprinkled with sea salt and herbs.

NOTE Harissa, a North African condiment made from roasted or dried chiles, salt, olive oil, and other flavorings, has a smoky, mellow heat. It's sold in cans, jars, and tubes and can be found at many supermarkets. Use it instead of your usual hot sauce in any dish or cocktail, especially a Bloody Mary.

ASPARAGUS AND GRUYÈRE PUFF
Preheat oven to 400°F. Prepare pastry shell as directed in step 1. Trim 1½ pounds **asparagus** spears to fit inside border; reserve. Bake crust until golden, about 15 minutes. Top with 2 cups shredded **Gruyère cheese** (6 ounces). Arrange asparagus in a single layer over cheese. Brush with 1 tablespoon **extra-virgin olive oil**, and season with **coarse salt** and freshly gound **pepper**. Bake until cheese has melted and spears are tender, about 20 minutes. Serve warm.

POTATO AND ROSEMARY PUFF
Preheat oven to 400°F. Prepare pastry shell as directed in step 1. Brush 1 tablespoon **extra-virgin olive oil** inside border. Toss 1 very thinly sliced **Yukon Gold potato** (unpeeled) with 1 tablespoon extra-virgin olive oil, and arrange evenly over pastry. Sprinkle with 2 tablespoons **fresh rosemary** leaves, and generously season with **coarse salt** and freshly ground **pepper**. Bake until crust and potatoes are golden brown, about 20 minutes. Drizzle with more oil, and serve warm.

SERVE ALL WITH

Stuffed Mushrooms (any variation; pages 212–215)

Glazed-Bacon Bites (page 73)

Lamb Meatballs with Harissa (page 154)

One, two, three, four—the greater the variety of meatballs, the better! All freeze well and take little time to prepare. We expanded on the most familiar options—Italian and Swedish meatballs (shown opposite, far left and right, respectively), served with their signature sauces—with two more versions, one lamb and one turkey (middle left and right), inspired by the flavors of Asia and North Africa.

Meatballs

ITALIAN MEATBALLS
makes 36

—

1 can (28 ounces) whole peeled tomatoes with juice

¼ cup plus 1 teaspoon extra-virgin olive oil

¾ teaspoon minced garlic

⅛ teaspoon red-pepper flakes

Coarse salt and freshly ground black pepper

1 slice white bread, crust removed

¼ cup warm milk

8 ounces ground pork

8 ounces lean ground beef

½ cup finely grated Parmigiano-Reggiano cheese, plus more for serving

1 large egg

1 tablespoon finely chopped fresh flat-leaf parsley leaves

1 tablespoon finely chopped shallot

¼ teaspoon dried marjoram

MAKE AHEAD Once meatballs are formed at end of step 3, freeze them in a single layer on a rimmed baking sheet until firm, about 1 hour. Then transfer to airtight containers or resealable plastic bags, and freeze up to 3 months. No need to thaw before proceeding with recipe.

1. Pulse tomatoes and their juice in a blender until almost smooth.

2. In a large skillet, heat 1 tablespoon oil, ½ teaspoon garlic, and red-pepper flakes over medium until garlic is sizzling, about 30 seconds. Stir in tomatoes, and season with salt. Reduce heat to low; simmer 30 minutes.

3. Meanwhile, soak bread in warm milk until absorbed, then squeeze out excess milk and discard. Finely chop bread; place in a large bowl. Add pork, beef, cheese, egg, parsley, shallot, marjoram, 1 teaspoon oil, remaining ¼ teaspoon garlic, ½ teaspoon salt, and ⅛ teaspoon black pepper. Using hands, gently mix to combine, then form into 1-inch balls.

4. Heat remaining 3 tablespoons oil in a large skillet over medium-high. Working in batches, cook meatballs until browned all over. Transfer to sauce, and simmer until cooked through, about 5 minutes more. Serve warm, sprinkled with more cheese.

SERVE WITH

Frico (page 14)

Ricotta Crostini (page 50) or Bruschetta (pages 133–135)

Burrata with Hot Pickled Peppers (page 61)

Marinated Zucchini with Mint and/or Marinated Artichoke Hearts (page 119)

Meatball Variations

LAMB WITH HARISSA
makes 36

- ¼ cup couscous
- ¼ cup boiling water
- 2 pitted dates
- 1 small onion, minced
- 3 tablespoons toasted pine nuts (see page 242)
- ½ cup chopped fresh cilantro leaves, plus whole leaves for serving
- 1 pound ground lamb
- ½ teaspoon ground allspice
- 1¼ teaspoons coarse salt
- 1 tablespoon extra-virgin olive oil

  Harissa, for serving

1. In a heatproof bowl, cover couscous with the boiling water. Cover and let stand 5 minutes, then drain. Meanwhile, soak dates in warm water to cover until plump, about 10 minutes; drain, chop, and place in a large bowl. Add onion, pine nuts, chopped cilantro, couscous, lamb, allspice, and salt. Using hands, gently mix to combine, then form into 1-inch balls.

2. Heat oil in a skillet over medium-high. Working in batches, cook meatballs until browned all over and cooked through, about 9 minutes. Serve warm, garnished with cilantro leaves and with harissa alongside.

SERVE WITH

Tortilla Española (page 129)

Harissa and Goat Cheese
Puff Tart (page 151)

Hummus (page 143) or
Muhammara (page 142) with
Spice-Rubbed Pita Crisps
(page 142)

ASIAN-STYLE TURKEY
makes 36

- ¾ cup plain fresh breadcrumbs (see page 242)
- 1½ pounds ground dark-meat turkey (93% lean)
- 3 scallions, white and pale-green parts finely chopped, dark-green parts thinly sliced, for serving
- ⅓ cup chopped fresh cilantro leaves
- 1 tablespoon plus 1 teaspoon fish sauce, such as nam pla
- 1 tablespoon plus 1 teaspoon Sriracha
- 1 tablespoon plus 1 teaspoon sugar
- 1 garlic clove, minced
- 1½ teaspoons coarse salt
- 1 tablespoon safflower oil

  Lime wedges, for serving

1. Preheat oven to 450°F. Combine breadcrumbs and 3 tablespoons water in a large bowl, and let stand 5 minutes. Add turkey, chopped scallion, cilantro, fish sauce, Sriracha, sugar, garlic, and salt. Using hands, gently mix to combine, then form into 1-inch balls.

2. Heat oil in a skillet over medium-high. Working in batches, cook meatballs until golden brown all over. Transfer to a rimmed baking sheet with a slotted spoon, and bake until cooked through, about 10 minutes more. Serve warm, with lime wedges and garnished with scallion greens.

SERVE WITH

Miso-Honey Wings
(page 125)

Vegetable Summer Rolls
(page 165)

Pork and Chive Pot Stickers
(page 166)

SWEDISH
makes 36

---

8 ounces ground sirloin

8 ounces ground pork

1 small onion, finely chopped

½ cup sour cream

1 large egg, lightly beaten

3 tablespoons plain dried breadcrumbs (see page 242)

1½ teaspoons coarse salt

½ teaspoon freshly ground pepper

½ teaspoon ground allspice

¼ teaspoon ground nutmeg

1 tablespoon safflower oil

2 tablespoons dry red wine, such as Pinot Noir

2 tablespoons all-purpose flour

2 cups low-sodium beef broth

¼ cup coarsely chopped fresh flat-leaf parsley

1. Preheat oven to 225°F. Combine beef, pork, onion, sour cream, egg, breadcrumbs, salt, pepper, and spices in a large bowl. Using hands, gently mix to combine, then form into 1-inch balls. Freeze on a rimmed baking sheet 30 minutes. Reroll in hands.

2. Heat oil in a skillet over medium-high. Working in batches, cook meatballs until browned all over and cooked through, about 6 minutes. Transfer to a rimmed baking sheet, and keep warm in oven while preparing sauce.

3. Pour off fat and large browned bits from skillet. Add wine to skillet; cook over medium heat, stirring, until mostly reduced. Whisk in flour, then add broth and parsley. Raise heat to medium-high. Simmer, stirring, until slightly thickened, 8 to 10 minutes. Strain through a fine sieve. Serve meatballs warm, topped with sauce.

SERVE WITH

Potato and Rosemary Puff (page 151) or **Provençal Onion Tart** (page 80)

Salmon Sliders (page 114)

Smoked Salmon on Rye Canapés (any variation; page 176)

Lemon-Parsley Gougères (page 46)

Here's an excellent reason to visit a local greenmarket or farm stand during the summer: the freshest tomatoes, wax beans, herbs, radicchio, and little potatoes—even eggs— under the sun, all available and ready to be assembled into a build-your-own grand aioli platter. Match the season's finest with the best-quality oil-packed tuna, olives, and bread you can find, alongside homemade sauces for dipping, such as the three classic French ones here. You'll want to chill a couple of bottles of Rosé, too.

Farm Stand Grand Aioli

ALMOND-MINT PESTO
makes 1 cup

Pulse 2 ounces (about ½ cup) chopped toasted blanched **almonds** (see page 242) and 2 chopped **shallots** in a food processor until a coarse paste forms. Add 2 cups loosely packed **fresh mint** leaves; pulse a few times until coarsely chopped. Add 1 cup finely grated **Parmigiano-Reggiano cheese** and 3 tablespoons **extra-virgin olive oil**; pulse a few times until combined. Season with **coarse salt** and freshly ground **pepper**.

MUSTARD VINAIGRETTE
makes 1 cup

Combine ¼ cup minced **shallot**, ¼ cup **white-wine vinegar**, 1 tablespoon plus 1 teaspoon **Dijon mustard**, and ½ teaspoon **coarse salt** in a bowl; let stand 15 minutes. Add 1 cup **extra-virgin olive oil** in a steady stream, whisking constantly, until emulsified. Vinaigrette can be refrigerated, covered, up to 2 days; whisk to combine before serving.

LEMON AIOLI
makes 1½ cups

Chop 2 **garlic** cloves. Add a pinch of **coarse salt.**
Mash into a paste with the flat side of a chef's knife.

Whisk 2 large room-temperature **egg** yolks with
½ teaspoon salt in a bowl. Slowly add 2 tablespoons
fresh **lemon** juice and 1 tablespoon **water,** whisking
until thoroughly blended. Add ¼ cup **extra-virgin
olive oil,** drop by drop, whisking until emulsified.
Whisk in another 1½ cups oil in a steady stream.
Stir in garlic paste.

NOTE See page 180 for how to
make perfect hard-boiled eggs
and page 53 for how to blanch
the string beans.

To cook new potatoes, cover
them with water by 2 inches
in a saucepan; bring to a boil,
then reduce heat, add salt, and
simmer until just tender, about
8 minutes. Let cool before slicing
about ¼ inch thick (halve smallest
ones).

One very flavorful dough plus three different, equally delicious fillings—chicken and kale, sausage and apple, and (vegetarian) cauliflower and manchego—means there's something to please host and guest alike. Because this dough is "short," with a higher percentage of fat to flour, it is rich and tender and super easy to work with (important when making dozens at once). See page 160 for make-ahead information.

Hand Pies

SAUSAGE AND APPLE
makes 16

▬

For the dough

4½ cups all-purpose flour, plus more for dusting

1 cup shredded cheddar cheese

1½ cups (3 sticks) cold unsalted butter, cut into small pieces

2 teaspoons coarse salt

¼ teaspoon sugar

2 large egg yolks

1 large egg whisked with 1 tablespoon heavy cream, for egg wash

For the filling

1 tablespoon extra-virgin olive oil

1½ links (10 ounces) sweet Italian sausage, removed from casings

1 onion, finely chopped

1 tart apple, such as Granny Smith, peeled, cored, and finely chopped

¼ cup golden raisins

Coarse salt and freshly ground pepper

SERVE ALL WITH

Winter Crudités with Buttermilk Dip (page 54)

Stuffed Mushrooms (any variation; pages 212–15)

Hot Artichoke Dip (page 68)

1. Make the dough: Pulse together flour, cheese, butter, salt, and sugar in a food processor until mixture resembles coarse meal. Add yolks; pulse to combine. With processor running, drizzle in ½ cup cold water until dough just comes together. (If dough is still crumbly, add up to ¼ cup more water, 1 tablespoon at a time.) Do not process more than 20 seconds. Divide mixture between two pieces of plastic wrap. Wrap in plastic. Refrigerate until firm, about 30 minutes and up to 1 day.

2. On a floured work surface, roll out dough to ¼ inch thick. With a 3½-inch biscuit cutter (or an inverted glass and paring knife), cut out 32 rounds. Arrange on parchment-lined baking sheet between layers of parchment, and cover with plastic wrap. Refrigerate rounds, at least 1 hour and up to 1 day.

3. Make the filling: Heat the oil in a large skillet over medium-high. Add sausage, and cook, breaking up meat with a spoon, until browned, about 5 minutes. Add onion, and cook until soft, stirring occasionally, about 6 minutes. Add apple and raisins. Cook, stirring occasionally, until apple is tender, about 5 minutes. Remove from heat; season with salt and pepper. Let cool.

4. Place 2 tablespoons sausage mixture on half of dough rounds, leaving a ½-inch border. Brush edges with egg wash, top with remaining dough rounds, and press with a fork to seal. Cut a vent in center, then brush egg wash over tops. Refrigerate until firm, about 30 minutes.

5. Preheat oven to 350°F. Bake until crust is golden brown, rotating sheet halfway through, about 30 minutes. Serve warm or at room temperature.

Fillings for Hand Pies

ROASTED CAULIFLOWER AND MANCHEGO
makes 16

—

1 small head cauliflower, florets separated and thinly sliced (about 4 cups)

¼ cup plus 3 tablespoons extra-virgin olive oil

Coarse salt and freshly ground pepper

⅔ cup toasted blanched hazelnuts (see page 242)

1 garlic clove

1 teaspoon finely grated lemon zest

2 teaspoons finely chopped fresh rosemary leaves

Dough for hand pies (page 159; use 1 cup shredded Manchego cheese in place of cheddar)

5 ounces Manchego cheese, thinly sliced

1. Preheat oven to 425°F. On a rimmed baking sheet, drizzle cauliflower with 3 tablespoons oil and season with salt and pepper. Toss to combine. Spread in a single layer. Roast until golden brown on bottom, about 7 minutes. Flip cauliflower; roast until other side is golden brown, about 5 minutes more. Let cool.

2. In a food processor, pulse hazelnuts and garlic until finely chopped. With processor running, slowly add remaining ¼ cup oil until combined. Add lemon zest and 1 teaspoon rosemary; season with salt and pepper. Process until chopped.

3. When forming pies as directed on page 159, spread 2 teaspoons hazelnut mixture onto half of dough rounds, leaving a ½-inch border. Dividing evenly, top with cauliflower, Manchego, and remaining teaspoon rosemary; season with pepper. Brush edges with egg wash, top with remaining dough rounds, and press to seal. Cut a vent in each, and chill before baking as directed.

MAKE AHEAD The dough can be frozen up to 3 months; let thaw overnight in the refrigerator before rolling out and cutting. The pies can be filled and formed, then frozen on baking sheet until firm. Transfer to resealable plastic bags, and freeze up to 1 month; bake (no need to thaw) for a few minutes longer.

CHICKEN AND KALE
makes 16

1 bone-in, skin-on chicken breast (about 1 pound)

1 small white onion, cut into wedges

1 dried bay leaf

1 tablespoon unsalted butter

1 leek, white and pale-green parts only, thinly sliced, washed well and drained

1 small bunch kale (8 ounces), preferably Tuscan, tough stems and ribs removed, coarsely chopped

1 teaspoon fresh thyme leaves

Coarse salt and freshly ground pepper

2 tablespoons all-purpose flour

1 cup low-sodium chicken broth

Dough for hand pies (page 159)

1. In a large saucepan, combine chicken, onion, and bay leaf with cold water to cover. Bring to a boil, then reduce heat and simmer until chicken is cooked through, about 15 minutes. Transfer to a plate; reserve 1 cup cooking liquid and discard onion and bay leaf. When chicken is cool enough to handle, shred into bite-size pieces (discard skin and bones).

2. In a large skillet, melt butter over medium-high heat. Add leek and cook, stirring, until soft, 3 minutes. Add kale and thyme and season with salt and pepper; cook, stirring occasionally, until kale wilts, about 3 minutes. Sprinkle flour over mixture and stir to combine. Add broth and bring to a boil. Cook, stirring often, until mixture thickens, about 2 minutes. Transfer to a bowl, season with salt and pepper, and stir in chicken. Let cool.

3. When forming pies as directed on page 159, divide chicken mixture among half of dough rounds, leaving a ½-inch border. Brush edges with egg wash, top with remaining rounds, and press to seal. Cut a vent in each, and chill before baking as directed.

Wrapped into handy bundles, summer rolls are tailor-made for fork-free eating. Once you've tackled the cooking, if any, for the fillings—shrimp, vegetable, or pork in this trio—these rolls are quick to assemble, even on the first try. Each of the dipping sauces pairs nicely with any of the rolls.

Summer Rolls

Summer Rolls

SHRIMP SUMMER ROLLS
makes 20

▬

1 pound medium shrimp (30 to 35), in shells

8 ounces rice vermicelli (rice-stick noodles)

1 small head Napa cabbage, halved, cored, and thinly sliced

5 carrots, peeled and cut into matchsticks

20 rice-paper wrappers (spring-roll skins)

1 bunch basil, preferably Thai basil

1 English cucumber or 4 Persian cucumbers, cut into thin spears

Peanut Dipping Sauce and Nuoc Cham Dipping Sauce (page 244), for serving

1. Bring 1 inch water to a boil in a large, deep straight-sided skillet. Submerge shrimp; immediately remove from heat and cover. Let stand 3 minutes; drain. Let cool and peel. Cut in half lengthwise and devein. Shrimp can be refrigerated, covered, up to 1 day.

2. Place vermicelli in a baking dish and cover with 1 inch hot water. Let stand until water is tepid, about 30 minutes; drain. Vermicelli can be refrigerated, covered, up to 1 day.

3. Meanwhile, submerge cabbage and carrots in 2 separate bowls of ice water for 30 minutes; drain.

SERVE ALL WITH

Miso-Honey Wings (page 125) or Ginger-Scallion Wings (page 125)

Asian-Style Turkey Meatballs (page 154)

Pork and Chive Pot Stickers (page 166) or Red Curry Shrimp Dumplings (page 168)

4. Pour at least 1 inch warm water into a bowl slightly larger than wrappers. Submerge 1 wrapper in warm water until pliable but still firm, about 10 seconds. (Replace warm water as necessary.) Transfer to a plate.

5. Place 3 pieces of shrimp, cut side up, on a wrapper. Dividing evenly, top with basil, cabbage, carrots, cucumber, and noodles. Lift side of wrapper closest to you and fold it tightly over filling. Fold in both ends of wrapper, then roll tightly to seal. Cover with a damp kitchen towel. Repeat with remaining wrappers and filling. Serve with dipping sauces.

PORK SUMMER ROLLS
makes 20

▬

½ cup fish sauce, such as nam pla

¼ cup safflower oil

¼ cup unseasoned rice-wine vinegar

1 lemongrass stalk, smashed

2 garlic cloves, thinly sliced

1 piece (½-inch) fresh peeled ginger, thinly sliced

1 jalapeño chile, thinly sliced (ribs and seeds removed for less heat, if desired)

2 teaspoons freshly ground black pepper

1 pork tenderloin (about 1 pound), silver skin trimmed

8 ounces rice vermicelli (rice-stick noodles)

2 carrots, peeled and cut into matchsticks

½ small jicama, peeled and cut into matchsticks

20 rice-paper wrappers (spring-roll skins)

1 bunch basil, preferably Thai basil

Peanut Dipping Sauce and Nuoc Cham Dipping Sauce (page 244), for serving

1. In a bowl, combine fish sauce, oil, vinegar, lemongrass, garlic, ginger, chile, and black pepper. Transfer to a resealable plastic bag; add pork, seal, and refrigerate at least 3 hours or up to 1 day.

2. Place vermicelli in a baking dish and cover with 1 inch hot water. Let stand until water is tepid, about 30 minutes; drain. Vermicelli can be refrigerated, covered, up to 1 day.

3. Meanwhile, submerge carrots and jicama in 2 separate bowls of ice water for 30 minutes; drain.

4. Heat grill (or grill pan) to medium. (If using a charcoal grill, coals are ready when you can hold your hand 6 inches above grate for just 4 to 5 seconds.) Remove pork from marinade; discard marinade. Grill pork, turning as necessary, until a meat thermometer inserted into thickest part registers 145°F. Transfer to a cutting board. When cool enough to handle, thinly slice meat.

5. Pour at least 1 inch warm water into a bowl slightly larger than spring-roll skins. Submerge 1 skin in the water until pliable but still firm, about 10 seconds. (Replace warm water as necessary.) Transfer to a plate.

6. Dividing evenly, layer basil, pork, carrot, jicama, and noodles on a wrapper. Lift side of wrapper closest to you and fold it tightly over filling. Fold in both ends of wrapper, then roll tightly to seal. Cover with a damp kitchen towel. Repeat with remaining wrappers and filling. Serve with dipping sauces.

VEGETABLE SUMMER ROLLS
makes 20

▬

8   ounces rice vermicelli (rice-stick noodles)

1   head Napa cabbage, halved, cored, and thinly sliced

4   large carrots, peeled and cut into matchsticks

20   rice-paper wrappers (spring-roll skins)

1   bunch basil, preferably Thai basil

2   English cucumbers or 4 Persian cucumbers, cut into thin spears

4   red bell peppers, ribs and seeds removed, cut into matchsticks

    Peanut Dipping Sauce and Nuoc Cham Dipping Sauce (page 244), for serving

1. Place vermicelli in a baking dish and cover with 1 inch hot water. Let stand until water is tepid, about 30 minutes; drain. Vermicelli can be refrigerated, covered, up to 1 day.

2. Meanwhile, submerge cabbage and carrots in 2 separate bowls of ice water for 30 minutes; drain.

3. Pour at least 1 inch warm water into a bowl slightly larger than wrapper. Submerge 1 wrapper in warm water until pliable but still firm, about 10 seconds. (Replace warm water as necessary.) Transfer to a plate.

4. Dividing evenly, layer basil, cucumber, carrot, bell pepper, cabbage, and noodles on a wrapper. Lift side of wrapper closest to you and fold it tightly over filling. Fold in both ends of wrapper, then roll tightly to seal. Cover with a damp kitchen towel. Repeat with remaining wrappers and filling. Serve with dipping sauces.

TIP To make summer rolls with scallion "skewers," as shown on pages 162 and 163, place a trimmed scallion on top of filling, in the center, leaving an inch or two extending beyond the edge of wrapper. Then proceed to fold and form the rolls.

Thanks to store-bought wonton wrappers (and other Asian ingredients, such as toasted sesame oil and curry paste), it's easier to make dumplings at home than you might think. This selection offers a nice contrast of shapes, textures, and flavors—one is steamed, the rest fried—and is served with the same delectable dipping sauce.

Dumplings

PORK AND CHIVE POT STICKERS
makes 40

—

½ pound ground pork

2 tablespoons minced fresh chives

1 tablespoon soy sauce

1 tablespoon dry sherry

2 teaspoons minced peeled fresh ginger (from a 1-inch piece)

1 teaspoon toasted sesame oil

1 teaspoon cornstarch

40 round wonton wrappers

2 tablespoons safflower oil

Soy-Ginger Dipping Sauce (page 168)

1. In a bowl, combine pork, chives, soy sauce, sherry, ginger, sesame oil, cornstarch, and 1 tablespoon water. Working with one wonton wrapper at a time, place 1 heaping teaspoon of pork mixture in center. Moisten edge of wrapper with water, fold over to form a half-moon shape, and press to seal.

2. Working in two batches, cook dumplings in a large pot of boiling water until just cooked through, about 4 minutes. Transfer to a plate with a slotted spoon.

3. In a large pan, heat safflower oil over medium-high. Again in two batches, cook until browned, about 1½ minutes per side. Serve dumplings immediately with dipping sauce.

MAKE AHEAD Dumplings can be filled and formed up to 1 month ahead; freeze on parchment-lined baking sheets until firm, about 1 hour, then transfer to resealable plastic bags and keep in the freezer.

Thaw the shrimp dumplings overnight in the refrigerator before cooking; because the pot stickers are boiled before frying, they do not need to be thawed.

Dumplings

SOY-GINGER DIPPING SAUCE
makes about 2 cups

---

1 cup low-sodium soy sauce

¾ cup unseasoned rice vinegar

¼ cup minced peeled fresh ginger (from a 4-inch piece)

3 tablespoons sugar

1 teaspoon toasted sesame oil

Stir together all ingredients in a bowl until sugar is dissolved. Sauce can be refrigerated, covered, up to 1 day; bring to room temperature and stir to combine before serving.

RED CURRY SHRIMP DUMPLINGS
makes 48

---

1 tablespoon plus 1 teaspoon safflower oil

¼ cup minced peeled fresh ginger (from a 4-inch piece)

4 scallions, very thinly sliced, plus julienned scallion greens, for garnish (optional)

1½ pounds large shrimp (24 to 30), peeled and deveined, finely chopped

3 tablespoons Thai red curry paste

2 teaspoons fish sauce, such as nam pla

48 square wonton wrappers

   Soy-Ginger Dipping Sauce (left)

1. In a small skillet, heat 2 teaspoons oil over medium-high. Cook ginger and scallions, stirring, until softened, about 2 minutes. Transfer to a bowl; add shrimp, curry paste, and fish sauce; stir to combine.

2. Working with one wrapper at a time, place 1 heaping teaspoon shrimp mixture in center. Moisten edges of wrapper, then bring all 4 corners together, pinching at top to seal.

3. In a large skillet, heat remaining 2 teaspoons oil over medium-high. Add dumplings, pinched-side up, and cook until golden brown on bottom, about 1 minute. Add ½ cup water, cover, and cook until dumplings are tender, about 3 minutes. Uncover; cook until water evaporates, about 1 minute. Garnish with scallion greens and serve immediately with dipping sauce.

CHICKEN AND THAI BASIL POT STICKERS
makes 40

—

- 2 ounces cellophane (or glass) noodles, blanched and chopped
- 1 pound ground chicken
- 1 cup coarsely grated peeled carrots (from 4 to 5 carrots)
- ¼ cup fresh basil, preferably Thai basil, finely chopped
- 4 scallions, green parts only, thinly sliced on the diagonal
- 1 garlic clove, minced
- 1 tablespoon Thai green curry paste
- 3 tablespoons fish sauce, such as nam pla
- 2 tablespoons plus 1½ teaspoons sugar
- 3 tablespoons coconut milk
  Coarse salt and freshly ground pepper
- 40 round wonton wrappers
  Soy–Ginger Dipping Sauce (opposite)

1. Place noodles in a bowl, add boiling water to cover, and let soak until tender, about 15 minutes. Drain well, then pat dry and coarsely chop.

2. Combine chicken, noodles, carrots, basil, scallions, garlic, curry paste, fish sauce, sugar, and coconut milk in a bowl. Season with salt and pepper.

3. Working with one wonton wrapper at a time, place a heaping teaspoon of chicken mixture in center. Moisten edge of wrapper with water, fold over to form a half-moon shape, and press to seal.

4. Working in two batches, cook dumplings in a large pot of boiling water until just cooked through, about 4 minutes. Transfer to a plate with a slotted spoon.

5. In a large pan, heat oil over medium-high. Again in two batches, cook until browned, 1 to 2 minutes per side. Serve immediately with dipping sauce.

SERVE ALL WITH

Beef and Asparagus Negimaki (page 84)

Asian-Style Turkey Meatballs (page 154)

Ginger-Scallion Wings (page 125) or **Miso-Honey Wings** (page 125)

Summer Rolls (any variation; pages 162–165)

Swap out the traditional stacked tiers for simple rustic galvanized tins, and fruits de mer—the French mixed-seafood classic—is instantly more approachable for the host (but still as spectacular for the lucky guests). Limiting the selection also helps; oysters, mussels, shrimp, and pre-cooked crab (claws and legs) are all that's needed for an eye-catching arrangement. Let the fishmongers do more of the prep work, if you prefer—many will shuck, steam, and handle other preparations for a nominal charge.

Fruits de Mer Platter

—

serves 6 to 8

12 raw oysters

12 jumbo head-on shrimp (2 pounds)

1 pound New Zealand mussels (12 to 16)

5 pounds frozen cooked Alaskan king crab legs, thawed

2 pounds frozen cooked snow crab claws, thawed

Serving Sauces (recipes follow)

Lemon wedges and hot sauce, for serving

1. Scrub oysters with a brush under cold running water. Holding oyster cupped side down, use an oyster knife to pry into oyster's hinge; twist knife to pop off top shell. Detach flesh from top shell, and scoop under oyster to loosen it from bottom shell.

2. Place a steamer basket (or colander) in a small pot filled with 2 inches water; bring to a boil, then reduce to a simmer. Place shrimp in basket; cover and steam until pink and opaque throughout, about 3 minutes. Plunge into an ice-water bath until cool.

3. Remove beards from mussels; scrub with a brush under cold running water. Fill a skillet with ¼ inch water, and bring to a simmer; add mussels, cover, and steam until they open, 2 to 3 minutes. (Discard any unopened mussels.) Remove with a slotted spoon; remove top shell. Chill mussels, covered, up to 4 hours.

4. Arrange all shellfish on a platter filled with ice and serve with sauces, lemon wedges, and hot sauce alongside.

Serving Sauces

LEMON AIOLI (see recipe on page 157)

PEPPERCORN MIGNONETTE
makes 1¼ cups

—

Crush 2 tablespoons whole **pink peppercorns** with the flat side of a chef's knife. In a small bowl, stir together ⅔ cup minced **shallot**, peppercorns, and 1½ cups **champagne vinegar**.

DRAWN BUTTER WITH LEMON
makes 2 cups

—

Bring 1 pound (4 sticks) **unsalted butter** to a simmer in a small saucepan over low heat, stirring until melted. Remove from heat, and let milk solids sink to bottom. Skim foam from surface, then carefully pour off clear butter into a bowl, leaving solids behind. Stir ½ cup fresh **lemon** juice (from 3 lemons) into bowl. Use immediately.

TIP For the serving tray, buy crushed ice; or place a few cups of ice in a plastic bag, wrap in a dish towel, and crush using a rolling pin or a meat tenderizer or pulse in a food processor.

SERVE WITH

Potatoes with Mascarpone and Roe (page 25)

Puff Pastry Cheese Straws (page 57)

Stylish
Bites

Festive occasions call for pretty hors d'oeuvres that guests can sample—and savor—all evening long. Now is the time to splurge on a few luxurious ingredients and to fuss, more than ever, so that each morsel is as memorable as the next.

Potatoes with Caviar and Crème Fraîche

makes 28

28 small red potatoes

½ cup plus 2 tablespoons milk

1 tablespoon unsalted butter, plus 2 tablespoons melted, for brushing

¼ cup crème fraîche

Coarse salt and freshly ground pepper

1 tablespoon minced fresh chives, plus more, cut into 1-inch lengths, for garnish (optional)

3 ounces caviar, such as sevruga or American sturgeon (paddlefish) caviar (about 2 tablespoons)

1. Cover potatoes in a large saucepan with cold water by 2 inches. Bring to a boil, then reduce heat and simmer until just knife-tender, 15 to 20 minutes. Drain potatoes.

2. When cool enough to handle, carefully cut off the very tops of potatoes. Using a melon baller or small spoon, scoop out as much flesh as possible into a large bowl, leaving a ¼-inch-thick border. Cut a small slice off the bottom of each potato shell so it will stand upright; arrange on a rimmed baking sheet.

3. Preheat oven to 375°F. In a small saucepan, heat milk and butter, stirring, until butter melts. Pass potato flesh through a ricer or wide-mesh sieve into a large bowl. Stir in warm milk mixture a little at a time until potato mixture is creamy. Stir in crème fraîche. Season with salt and pepper. Stir in chives.

4. Use a pastry bag fitted with a large plain tip to pipe potato filling into shells. Place on a rimmed baking sheet, and bake until golden brown and slightly puffed, about 15 minutes. Remove from oven, brush with melted butter, and bake 15 minutes more. Dividing evenly, top each potato with caviar and a piece of fresh chive (if using); serve immediately.

At parties from Scandinavia to New York, you'll find appetizers of smoked salmon (also known as lox) and rye. It's hard to beat the rich, salty flavor and the silky texture of the fish, which matches well with other flavors and textures from across the spectrum.

Smoked Salmon on Rye Canapés
—

makes 24

CREAM CHEESE, CAPER, AND RED ONION
Dividing evenly, spread 1 bar (8 ounces) **cream cheese**, room temperature, over 24 slices **party-size rye bread**. Top with 12 ounces thinly sliced **smoked salmon**; 2 tablespoons **capers**, drained and rinsed; and 1 small **red onion**, very thinly sliced.

SOFT SCRAMBLED EGG, AVOCADO, AND SCALLION
Melt 1 tablespoon unsalted **butter** in a large nonstick skillet over medium heat. Whisk together 8 large **eggs** in a bowl, then add to skillet. Cook until soft curds form, stirring with a flexible spatula to create curds and slide eggs from edges to center, 3 to 4 minutes. Transfer to a plate, and let cool completely. Dividing evenly, top 24 slices **party-size rye bread** with eggs, 12 ounces thinly sliced **smoked salmon**, 1 thinly sliced avocado, and thinly sliced **scallions** (from 1 bunch).

CRÈME FRAICHE, FISH ROE, AND CHIVE
Dividing evenly, top 24 slices **party-size rye bread** with 12 ounces thinly sliced **smoked salmon**, 8 ounces (1 cup) **crème fraîche**, 2 ounces (¼ cup) **fish roe**, such as salmon or trout roe, and **fresh chives**, cut into 1-inch lengths.

GOAT CHEESE, RADISH, AND WATERCRESS
Dividing evenly, spread 8 ounces soft **goat cheese**, room temperature, over 24 slices **party-size rye bread**. Top with 12 ounces thinly sliced **smoked salmon**, 1 bunch **radishes**, thinly sliced, and small **watercress** sprigs (from 1 bunch).

BUTTER, DILL, AND CUCUMBER
Dividing evenly, spread ½ cup (1 stick) **unsalted butter**, room temperature, over 24 slices **party-size rye bread**. Top with 12 ounces thinly sliced **smoked salmon**, 2 **kirby cucumbers**, thinly sliced; and small **dill** sprigs (from 1 bunch).

A classic never goes out of style. Take the deviled egg, that ever-popular finger food with a built-in base (the white) and endlessly adaptable filling (the yolk). Piping is a quick way to fill a lot of eggs at once, or you can simply use a spoon. Either way, these "dressed" eggs will make any occasion feel special. Our recipes include (from left to right): classic; tomato-pimentón; cucumber, dill, and caper; miso-Sriracha; wasabi-scallion; olive-garlic; and watercress-horseradish.

Deviled Eggs

Deviled Eggs

CLASSIC DEVILED EGGS
makes 16

—

8	large eggs
⅓	cup mayonnaise
1	tablespoon Dijon mustard
1	teaspoon white-wine vinegar
	Coarse salt and freshly ground pepper

1. In a saucepan, cover eggs with 1 inch of water. Bring to a boil; remove from heat. Cover and let stand 8 minutes. Drain eggs; run under cold water until cool enough to handle.

2. Peel eggs and halve lengthwise; remove yolks and transfer to a bowl. Mash with a fork, then mix in mayonnaise, mustard, and vinegar. Season with salt and pepper.

3. Fill whites with yolk mixture as desired (see note, below). Refrigerate until set, about 15 minutes or up to 2 hours.

NOTE Piping makes fast work of filling the egg whites, and you can use basic pastry tips to achieve lovely results. We are especially fond of plain tips, such as Ateco #805, and open-star tips, such as Ateco #824. You can also pipe the filling into the whites using a resealable plastic bag with a corner snipped off, or simply spoon it in.

TIPS FOR MAKING PERFECT HARD-BOILED EGGS

Start with slightly older eggs, which will be easier to peel after boiling than fresher ones. Eggs will keep up to 4 weeks past the "pack date" on the carton.

Peel eggs as soon as they are cool enough to handle, either under cold running water or in a bowl of cold water (the water helps separate the membrane from the egg white).

MAKE AHEAD You can store peeled eggs in a bowl of cold water in the refrigerator up to 1 day before halving.

Up to a day before serving, place the egg-white shells on a rimmed baking sheet lined with damp paper towels; cover with more damp paper towels and wrap well in plastic.

You can also prepare the fillings several hours ahead; refrigerate them in piping bags or resealable plastic bags (or airtight containers if not piping them into the shells).

Fillings for Deviled Eggs

TOMATO-PIMENTÓN
Prepare classic deviled eggs, stirring 2 teaspoons **tomato paste** and 1 teaspoon **sweet smoked paprika** (dulce pimentón) into yolk mixture. Fill whites with yolk mixture. Garnish with more paprika.

CUCUMBER, DILL, AND CAPERS
Prepare classic deviled eggs; omit mayonnaise and vinegar from yolk mixture, and reduce mustard to ½ teaspoon. Stir ¼ cup plain **Greek yogurt**, 1 tablespoon chopped **fresh dill**, 2 tablespoons chopped **capers**, and ½ **English cucumber**, peeled and diced, into yolk mixture. Season with **coarse salt** and freshly ground **pepper**. Fill whites with yolk mixture. Garnish with dill sprigs.

MISO-SRIRACHA
Prepare classic deviled eggs, stirring 1 teaspoon low-sodium **soy sauce**, 4 teaspoons **miso paste**, and 1 teaspoon **Sriracha** into yolk mixture. Fill whites with yolk mixture. Garnish with **black sesame seeds**.

WASABI-SCALLION
Prepare classic deviled eggs; omit mustard, white-wine vinegar, and pepper from yolk mixture. Stir 1½ teaspoons **wasabi paste**, 2 teaspoons **rice-wine vinegar**, and 2 minced large **scallions** (3 tablespoons) into yolk mixture. Fill whites with yolk mixture. Garnish with **pea shoots** or sprouts.

OLIVE-GARLIC
Prepare classic deviled eggs, pulsing yolk mixture with 3 tablespoons finely chopped pitted **olives** and 1 small minced **garlic** clove in a food processor. Fill whites with yolk mixture. Garnish with olive slivers.

WATERCRESS-HORSERADISH
Prepare classic deviled eggs, stirring ¾ cup finely chopped **watercress** and 2 teaspoons drained prepared **horseradish** into yolk mixture. Fill whites with yolk mixture. Garnish with watercress leaves.

A double dose of sharp cheeses—cheddar and Gruyère—makes addictive crackers that don't even need a topping, but we like them with a little pepper jelly or quince paste. The same goes for our other two versions (recipes on page 184): The whole-wheat crackers pair perfectly with creamy cheeses like Taleggio or Brie and pear or apple, and the almond crackers flecked with chopped port-soaked figs work beautifully with soft, mild ricotta or pungent blue cheese and a drizzle of honey. All three doughs come together quickly—and keep in the freezer for months.

Slice-and-Bake Crackers

CHEDDAR-AND-GRUYÈRE
makes about 72

▬

2 cups all-purpose flour

2 teaspoons coarse salt

1 teaspoon poppy seeds, plus more for topping

4 tablespoons cold unsalted butter, cut into small pieces

1 cup finely shredded sharp cheddar cheese

1 cup finely shredded Gruyère cheese

½ cup whole milk

½ teaspoon Dijon mustard

Hot-pepper jelly, for serving (optional)

1. In a bowl, whisk together flour, salt, and poppy seeds. Work in butter with your fingers or a pastry blender until crumbly. Stir in cheeses. Whisk together milk and mustard; stir into flour mixture with a fork until dough forms. Divide in half; shape each into a 2-inch-wide log. Wrap in plastic; freeze at least 1 hour.

2. Preheat oven to 350°F. Cut logs into ⅛-inch-thick rounds; arrange on parchment-lined baking sheets, and sprinkle with poppy seeds. Bake until edges are golden, rotating sheets once, 14 to 16 minutes. Let crackers cool on sheets on a wire rack before topping with jelly and serving.

MAKE AHEAD Wrapped well in plastic, the logs of dough will keep for up to 3 months in the freezer. Let the frozen dough stand at room temperature for about 10 minutes to soften a bit before slicing (longer if dough starts to crack). A sharp chef's knife is the best tool to use.

Baked crackers can be stored in an airtight container at room temperature up to 5 days.

Slice-and-Bake Cracker Variations

FIG-AND-ALMOND
makes about 72

—

16 dried Black Mission figs, finely chopped

½ cup port

1 cup almonds

2 cups all-purpose flour

2 teaspoons coarse salt

½ cup (1 stick) cold unsalted butter, cut into small pieces

Fresh ricotta cheese and clover honey, for serving (optional)

1. In a bowl, soak figs in port 10 minutes.

2. In a food processor, pulse almonds, flour, and salt until finely ground. Add butter; pulse just until crumbly. Transfer to a bowl; stir in figs and port with a fork until dough forms. Divide in half; shape each into a 2-inch-wide log. Wrap in plastic; freeze at least 1 hour or up to 3 months.

3. Preheat oven to 350°F. Cut logs into ⅛-inch-thick rounds; arrange on parchment-lined baking sheets. Bake until edges are golden, rotating sheets halfway through, 14 to 16 minutes. Let crackers cool completely on sheets on a wire rack before topping with cheese and honey and serving.

WHOLE-WHEAT-AND-SESAME
makes about 72

—

2 cups whole-wheat flour

¼ cup sesame seeds, plus more for topping

¼ cup sugar

1½ teaspoons coarse salt

½ cup (1 stick) cold unsalted butter, cut into small pieces

½ cup heavy cream

Flaky sea salt, such as Maldon, for topping

Taleggio cheese, sliced pear, and freshly ground pepper, for serving (optional)

1. In a bowl, whisk together flour, sesame seeds, sugar, and coarse salt. Work in butter with your fingers or a pastry blender until crumbly. Stir in cream with a fork until dough forms. Divide in half; shape each into a 2-inch-wide log. Wrap in plastic; freeze at least 1 hour or up to 3 months.

2. Preheat oven to 350°F. Cut logs into ⅛-inch-thick rounds; arrange on parchment-lined baking sheets, and sprinkle with sesame seeds and sea salt. Bake until edges are golden, rotating sheets halfway through, 14 to 16 minutes. Let crackers cool completely on sheets on a wire rack before topping with cheese, pear, and pepper and serving.

A mixture of chopped hard-cooked eggs, crème fraîche, and minced chives gets topped with a colorful layer of trout roe for a salty, surprising pop. Serve with crackers, crostini, or sturdy potato chips—and a crisp, dry Champagne.

Egg-and-Caviar Dip

serves 6 to 8

12 large eggs

½ cup crème fraîche

3 tablespoons minced fresh chives

½ teaspoon coarse salt

½ teaspoon Dijon mustard

6 ounces trout roe

1. In a large saucepan, cover eggs with 1 inch of water. Bring to a boil; remove from heat. Cover and let stand 8 minutes. Drain eggs; run under cold water until cool enough to handle. Peel eggs.

2. Combine all ingredients except roe in a bowl; spread evenly in a 9-inch gratin dish or pie dish. Top with roe in a single layer. Serve immediately with crackers.

Endive spears and cucumber rounds aren't the least bit dainty when topped with a substantial, flavorful salad, such as curried egg, tuna and white bean, and shrimp and avocado. All provide a nice bit of protein, but in light, fresh packages. Any of the salads can be used to top cucumber or endive, so feel free to mix and match.

Cucumber and Endive Salad Bites

SHRIMP AND AVOCADO SALAD
makes about 60

Working in batches, boil 2 pounds medium **shrimp** (50 to 60), peeled and deveined (see page 242), in a large pot of salted boiling water until pink and opaque, about 1 minute. Remove with a slotted spoon, and let cool. Cut into ¼-inch pieces; place in a bowl. Stir in 2 tablespoons fresh **lime** juice, ¼ cup finely chopped **scallions**, 2 finely chopped **jalapeño chiles** (ribs and seeds removed if less heat is desired), and 2 teaspoons **coarse salt**. Refrigerate at least 30 minutes or up to 2 hours.

Just before serving, peel 1 ripe but firm **avocado** and cut into ¼-inch cubes. Gently fold into shrimp mixture. Dividing evenly, top **cucumber** slices or **endive** spears (see note, below) with shrimp salad; garnish with thinly sliced **scallion** greens.

NOTE You will need 2 English cucumbers, cut ¼ inch thick on the diagonal, to yield 64 slices, and about 8 heads Belgian endive to get 64 leaves. Prepare these just before serving.

TUNA AND WHITE BEAN SALAD
makes about 60

In a large bowl, toss together 2 jars (6.7 ounces each) oil-packed **tuna**, drained, 1 can (15.5 ounces) **navy beans**, drained and rinsed, 2 minced **garlic** cloves, 4 diced **plum tomatoes**, 3 tablespoons **extra-virgin olive oil**, ¼ cup fresh **lemon** juice, 2 tablespoons **capers**, rinsed and drained, and 1 cup coarsely chopped **fresh flat-leaf parsley** leaves. Season with **coarse salt** and freshly ground **pepper**. Dividing evenly, top **cucumber** slices or **endive** spears (see note, left) with tuna salad.

CURRIED EGG SALAD
makes about 60

Chop egg whites of 18 hard-boiled **eggs** (see page 180); crumble 6 yolks and reserve remaining yolks for another use. In a large bowl, mix egg whites and crumbled yolks, 2 diced **celery** stalks, 2 teaspoons **Dijon mustard**, ⅔ cup **mayonnaise**, and ½ teaspoon **curry powder**. Season with **coarse salt** and freshly ground **pepper**.

Dividing evenly, top **cucumber** slices or **endive** spears (see note, left) with egg salad; sprinkle with more pepper.

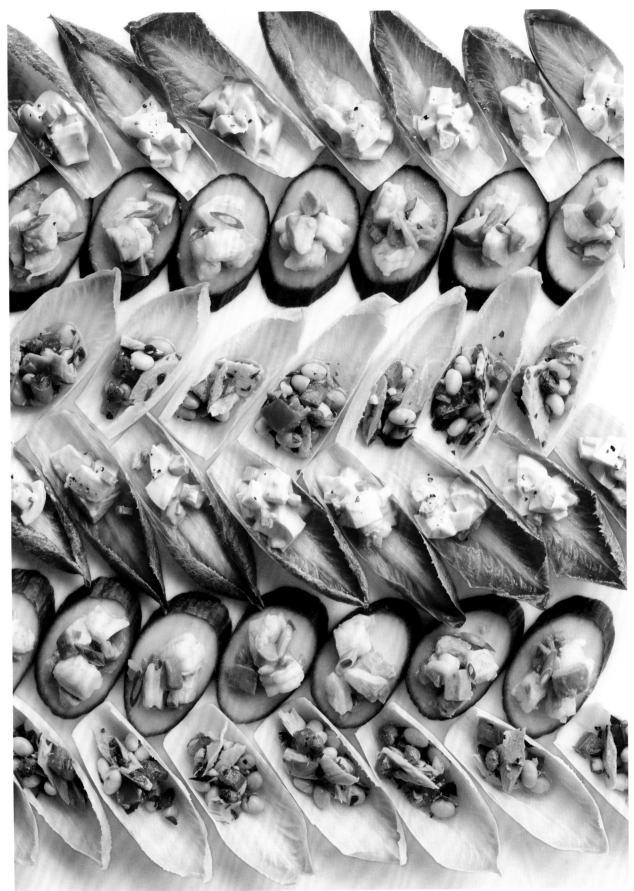

Blini—tiny Russian pancakes—make delightful bases for dollops of crème fraîche and spoonfuls of caviar (less expensive paddlefish and trout roes are shown here, and haddock roe is another option). In the spirit of tradition, these are made with buckwheat flour, for a distinctive nutty flavor and darker hue, and are served with shots of ice-cold vodka.

Blini with Crème Fraîche and Caviar

—

makes 30

1   envelope (2¼ teaspoons) active dry yeast

½   cup warm water (110˚F)

½   cup buckwheat flour

½   cup all-purpose flour

½   teaspoon coarse salt

¾   cup plain yogurt

1   tablespoon unsalted butter, melted

½   teaspoon sugar

2   large eggs, separated

    Crème fraîche, for serving

1   to 3 ounces caviar, for serving

1. In a small bowl, stir yeast into warm water; let stand until foamy, about 5 minutes. In another bowl, whisk together both flours and the salt. In a large bowl, stir together yogurt, butter, sugar, and egg yolks. Whisk in yeast mixture and flour mixture. Let batter stand, covered, in a warm spot, 30 minutes.

2. In a clean bowl, beat egg whites until stiff peaks form; fold whites into batter. Let stand 10 minutes.

3. Heat a 12-inch nonstick skillet over medium. Working in batches, add 1 tablespoon batter for each blini; cook until golden, about 2 minutes per side. Top each with a dollop of crème fraîche and some caviar (¼ to ½ teaspoon) and serve.

—

MAKE AHEAD You can cook blini up to 2 days in advance, and keep covered in the refrigerator. Or freeze on a baking sheet until firm, about 1 hour; then transfer to resealable plastic bags, and freeze up to 1 month. Reheat on a baking sheet (do not thaw), covered with parchment-lined foil, in a 350°F oven until warmed through, 10 to 15 minutes.

It's no surprise that scaled-down versions of quiche are a perennial favorite for caterers: They are easy to form in big batches using mini muffin tins, can be served at room temperature, and are incredibly versatile, partnering well with all kinds of fresh and flavorful ingredients. Ours include (third row, from left to right): mixed fresh herbs; cherry tomato and Pecorino; bacon and scallion; sautéed mushroom; caramelized onion and gorgonzola; and pureed pea and mint.

Mini Quiches

Mini Quiches

MINI QUICHES WITH MIXED FRESH HERBS
makes 48

■

For the crust

3½ cups all-purpose flour, plus more for dusting

2 teaspoons coarse salt

1 cup (2 sticks) cold unsalted butter, cut into pieces

2 large whole eggs, plus 2 large egg yolks

¼ cup plus 2 tablespoons ice water

For the filling

4 large eggs

1 cup heavy cream

1 cup milk

1 teaspoon coarse salt

¼ teaspoon freshly ground pepper

For the topping

½ cup packed mixed small herb sprigs, such as chervil and dill

1. Make the crust: In a food processor, pulse flour and salt until combined. Add butter and pulse just until mixture resembles coarse meal. In a bowl, whisk together eggs and yolks with ice water. Add to flour mixture, and pulse just until moist crumbs start to form (do not overmix). Transfer to a piece of plastic wrap, and, using wrap and your hands, form into a disk. Refrigerate until firm, at least 30 minutes and up to 4 hours.

2. Let dough sit at room temperature until pliable. On a lightly floured surface, roll out dough to slightly less than ⅛ inch thick. Using a 2¾-inch round cutter, cut out 48 rounds. Fit rounds into nonstick mini muffin tins. If dough becomes too soft to work with, refrigerate 15 minutes.

3. Preheat oven to 400°F. Place another mini muffin tin on top of tart shells (as a weight). Bake 10 minutes; remove top tin and bake until golden, about 5 minutes more. Let cool. Reduce oven temperature to 375°F.

4. Make the filling: In a bowl, whisk eggs until smooth, then whisk in cream, milk, salt, and pepper until well combined. Pour custard mixture into cooled crusts, stopping just short of top. (You may not need to use all of custard; be careful not to overfill.) Dividing evenly, top with herbs.

5. Bake 10 minutes; reduce oven to 325°F. Bake until filling is just set, about 10 minutes. Let cool in tin on a wire rack about 1 hour before turning out quiches and serving.

MAKE AHEAD The shells can be blind-baked (through step 3) up to 1 day ahead; let cool completely before wrapping in plastic and storing at room temperature, or freeze up to 3 months.

TIP If you don't have enough mini muffin tins, you can bake the shells in batches, then transfer to a parchment-lined rimmed baking sheet before baking the rest. Then fill the shells and bake the quiches on the baking sheet.

Fillings for Mini Quiches

PUREED PEA AND MINT

Prepare crust and filling. Place 1 cup **frozen green peas** (6 ounces) and 3 tablespoons packed **fresh mint** leaves in a steamer basket (or colander) set over a saucepan filled with 2 inches water; bring to a boil, then reduce to a simmer. Cover and steam until tender, about 2 minutes. Blend peas and mint with ⅓ cup steaming liquid until smooth; season with **coarse salt**. Mix into quiche filling and pour into crusts. Omit herb topping. Bake as directed. (This makes enough filling for 64 quiches.)

CHERRY TOMATO AND PECORINO

Prepare crust and mix ¼ cup plus 2 tablespoons finely grated **Pecorino cheese** into filling; pour into crusts. Omit herbs and, dividing evenly, top with ½ cup grated Pecorino cheese and 24 halved **cherry tomatoes,** cut side up. Bake as directed.

SAUTÉED MUSHROOM

Prepare crust and filling. Place ½ ounce dried **porcini mushrooms** in a bowl and add boiling water to cover. Let soften 30 minutes. Strain porcini through a cheesecloth-lined sieve, reserving ⅓ cup liquid. Stir porcini liquid into quiche filling until smooth. Melt 2 tablespoons **unsalted butter** in a skillet over medium-high. Cook 28 small **cremini mushrooms,** trimmed and sliced into thirds lengthwise, without stirring, until deep golden brown, about 5 minutes. Pour quiche filling into crusts. Omit herbs; top with mushroom slices and bake as directed. (This makes enough filling for 64 quiches.)

BACON AND SCALLION

Follow recipe through step 4, omitting herbs. While quiches are baking, cut 8 slices thick-cut **bacon** into ¼-inch dice and cook in a skillet over medium heat until browned, stirring frequently, about 10 minutes. Using a slotted spoon, transfer bacon to paper towels to drain. A few minutes before quiches have finished baking, sprinkle with bacon, dividing evenly, and continue baking until filling is just set, 2 to 3 minutes. Omit herbs; top with ½ cup thinly sliced **scallions,** dividing evenly, before serving.

CARAMELIZED ONION AND GORGONZOLA

Prepare crust and filling. Heat 1 tablespoon **extra-virgin olive oil** in a large skillet over low heat. Add 1 large **onion,** thinly sliced. Cook, stirring frequently, until golden brown, 20 to 25 minutes. Pour filling into crusts. Omit herb topping; dividing evenly, top quiches with onions and ½ cup crumbled **gorgonzola cheese** and bake as directed.

When is a ham-and-cheese sandwich much, much more than a ham-and-cheese sandwich? When it's the French classic that layers thin white bread (we used baguette-like *ficelle*) with béchamel sauce, thinly sliced ham, and Gruyère. These mini open-faced croques deliver all the deliciousness of the full-size version.

Croque-Monsieur Bites

—

makes 40

1 ficelle or thin baguette, cut into 40 slices (¼ inch thick)

1 tablespoon unsalted butter

1 tablespoon all-purpose flour

1 cup whole milk

2 tablespoons Dijon mustard

¼ teaspoon freshly grated nutmeg

Coarse salt and freshly ground pepper

1¾ cups shredded Gruyère cheese

6 ounces thinly sliced ham, cut into 40 (1-inch wide) strips

1. Preheat oven to 350°F. Arrange bread slices in a single layer on a rimmed baking sheet. Bake until lightly toasted, about 8 minutes. Transfer to a wire rack to cool.

2. Heat broiler with rack 6 inches from heat source. Melt butter in a saucepan over medium-high heat. Whisk in flour. Cook, whisking constantly, until mixture turns light golden, about 3 minutes. Slowly whisk in milk. Cook, whisking frequently, until sauce is thick enough to coat the back of a wooden spoon and hold a line drawn by your finger, about 5 minutes. Remove from heat. Stir in mustard and nutmeg; season with salt and pepper. Add 1 cup cheese, stirring until melted and smooth.

3. Arrange toasted bread on a rimmed baking sheet. Dividing evenly, spread béchamel on toasts; top with a slice of ham and then sprinkle with remaining ¾ cup cheese. Broil until sauce is bubbly and cheese is golden, 2 to 3 minutes. Serve warm.

Appetizer crepes begin in the traditional way: the artful swirl of the pan that results in a uniformly whisper-thin pancake. Each crepe is filled, rolled, and cut into bite-size portions. The display of three different fillings creates a striking visual: cucumber and fresh dill; salmon and capers; and the savory-sweet combination of ham and fruit jam.

Crepe Roll-Ups

makes 24

3½ cups milk

8 large eggs

6 tablespoons unsalted butter, melted and cooled, plus about 4 tablespoons, room temperature, for cooking crepes

2 cups all-purpose flour

1½ teaspoons coarse salt

2 bars (8 ounces each) cream cheese, room temperature

8 ounces fresh goat cheese, room temperature

Fillings (recipes follow)

1. Puree milk, eggs, cooled melted butter, flour, and salt in a blender until smooth. Transfer to a bowl, cover, and refrigerate at least 2 hours and up to 1 day.

2. Whisk batter until smooth. Melt ½ teaspoon butter in a 10-inch nonstick skillet or crepe pan over medium heat. Tilt skillet at a 45-degree angle, pour in a scant ¼ cup batter, and immediately swirl skillet in a circular motion to evenly distribute batter in a thin film across bottom. Cook until edges turn golden, about 45 seconds. Flip crepe and cook just until set, about 30 seconds. Transfer to a paper-towel-lined plate.

3. Melt another ½ teaspoon butter and continue cooking crepes in the same manner, whisking batter between crepes and stacking cooked crepes. Let crepes cool completely.

4. Mix together cream cheese and goat cheese in a bowl. Working with one crepe at a time, spread ¼ cup cheese mixture on top, almost to edge. Cut crepe into a half-moon, then top with desired filling. Roll up into a log. Place, seam side down, on a baking sheet. Repeat with remaining crepes and filling. Refrigerate 1 hour. Trim ends and cut logs into 1-inch-thick slices. Arrange on a platter. Refrigerate, covered, until ready to serve. Garnish as directed.

Fillings for Crepe Roll-Ups

CUCUMBER AND DILL

Thinly slice **English cucumbers** lengthwise. Sprinkle with **coarse salt**, and let drain in a colander 30 minutes. Pat dry. Top each crepe with 3 to 4 slices cucumber to cover; sprinkle with chopped **fresh dill** and finely grated **lemon** zest and roll up. Garnish with small dill sprigs.

SMOKED SALMON AND CAPERS

Top each crepe with 1 ounce thinly sliced **smoked salmon** pieces, then sprinkle with 2 teaspoons chopped **chives** and 1 teaspoon **capers** (drained and rinsed), and roll up. Garnish with more chives.

HAM AND JAM

Spread 2 teaspoons **apricot** or **fig jam** on each crepe, then layer with a thin slice of **ham** and roll up.

MAKE AHEAD The crepes can be refrigerated, wrapped in plastic, up to 2 days. To freeze, wrap them in paper towels (to absorb moisture when thawing) and then plastic, and place in a resealable plastic bag; freeze up to 1 month. Thaw before using.

Tostones, the succulent fried-plantain patties that are a specialty of the Caribbean, make a delicious base for a zesty crab-and-avocado salad. Double-frying produces crisp, golden brown results, and they'll stay that way for a couple of hours. Pair the tostones with any of our ceviches (see pages 208 to 211), and serve with Pisco Spritzes (page 236) or Piña Coladas (page 237).

Tostones with Crab Salad

—

makes 36

½ **pound jumbo lump crabmeat, picked over**

3 **tablespoons mayonnaise**

½ **ripe but firm avocado, pitted, peeled, and cut into ¼-inch dice (½ cup)**

2 **tablespoons fresh lime juice**

2 **tablespoons minced fresh chives**

Coarse salt

Safflower oil, for frying

3 **green plantains (see note, below), peeled and cut into ½-inch-thick slices**

2 **radishes, trimmed and cut into matchsticks, for garnish**

1. In a bowl, gently combine crabmeat, mayonnaise, avocado, lime juice, and chives; season with salt. Crab salad can be refrigerated, with plastic wrap pressed directly on surface, up to 8 hours.

2. Heat 2 inches oil in a heavy-bottomed pot over high until 350°F on a deep-fry thermometer. Working in 3 batches, fry plantains until golden all over, about 4 minutes. Using a slotted spoon, transfer to a paper-towel-lined plate. Return oil to 350°F between batches. Flatten warm plantains with a mallet until very thin.

3. Return oil to 350°F. In batches, fry plantains again until golden brown and crisp, about 3 minutes. Transfer to a paper-towel-lined baking sheet. Season with salt.

4. Top tostones with crab salad, dividing evenly, and garnish with radishes. Serve immediately.

NOTE Be sure to use only green plantains, which are firm and starchy and just right for frying; yellow or black ones will be too ripe and soft (similar to bananas).

MAKE AHEAD Fried tostones can be stored on the lined baking sheet at room temperature, uncovered, up to 2 hours.

Layers of complementary flavors and contrasting textures and colors—that's what gives canapés their enduring appeal. When making multiples, start with a range of breads and a gluten-free alternative or two, such as a rice cracker or potato chip. Cut the bread into circles, squares, or rectangles, and offer several types of toppings, including vegetarian options. Fourth row from top, left to right: fennel-crusted lamb on brioche; smoked trout, crème fraîche, and pickled onions on pumpernickel; black-olive butter and radishes on baguette; seared tuna with roe on rice crackers; and roasted wild mushrooms and goat cheese on rye.

Classic Canapés

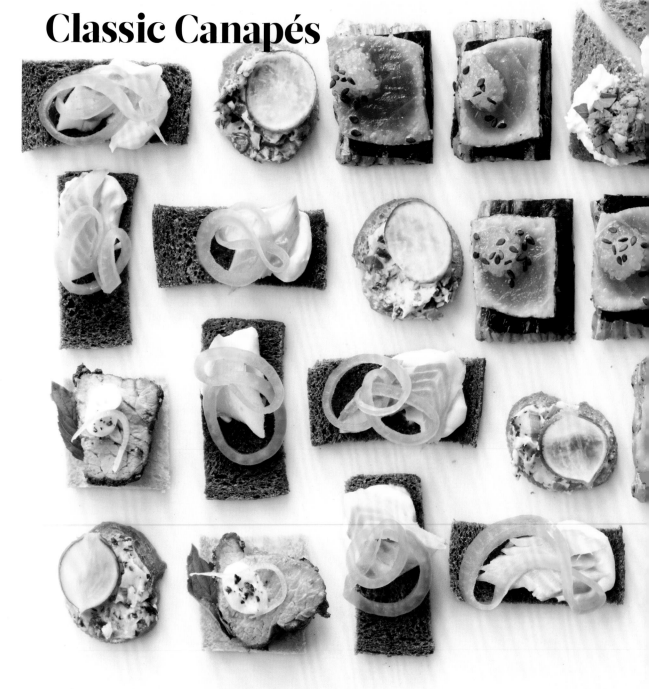

Classic Canapés

FENNEL-CRUSTED LAMB ON BRIOCHE
makes 36

2 teaspoons fennel seeds

1 pound boneless leg of lamb, trimmed of fat

Coarse salt and freshly ground pepper

1 loaf brioche bread, cut into ¼-inch-thick slices, then cut into 2-inch squares

¼ cup plain Greek yogurt

2 tablespoons extra-virgin olive oil

Peeled zest of 1 to 2 lemons (in long strips) plus 1 teaspoon fresh lemon juice

1 bunch fresh mint

1. Heat a small skillet over medium. Add fennel seeds, and toast, gently shaking pan, until fragrant, about 30 seconds. Transfer to a plate to cool.

2. Preheat oven to 350°F. Pound lamb to 1 inch thick with a meat mallet. Cut lengthwise into 1-inch-wide planks. Grind toasted fennel seeds in a spice mill (or clean coffee grinder). Combine with 1 teaspoon each salt and pepper in a small bowl. Reserve ½ teaspoon spice blend; sprinkle remaining all over lamb. Let stand 10 minutes.

3. Meanwhile, toast bread on a baking sheet until golden and crisp, 8 to 10 minutes. Let cool completely. In a bowl, whisk together yogurt, 1 tablespoon oil, ¼ teaspoon salt, and the lemon juice.

4. Heat a large sauté pan over medium-high. Swirl in remaining tablespoon oil. Working in batches, add lamb planks, at least 1 inch apart. Cook, turning, until browned on all four sides, about 1 minute per side. Transfer to a cutting board; let rest 10 minutes before slicing crosswise ¼ inch thick.

5. Top each toast with 1 mint leaf, a lamb slice, ¼ teaspoon yogurt mixture, reserved spice blend (dividing evenly), and a strip of lemon zest.

SEARED TUNA ON RICE CRACKERS WITH WHITEFISH ROE
makes 36

8 ounces cold sushi-grade tuna steak (1 inch thick)

Coarse salt and freshly ground pepper

½ cup mayonnaise

36 nori-wrapped rice crackers or sesame-rice crackers

Toasted sesame oil, for brushing

4 ounces whitefish roe or trout roe

Black sesame seeds, for sprinkling

1. Cut tuna lengthwise into 1¼-inch-wide planks. Heat a large skillet over medium-high. Season tuna generously all over with salt and pepper. Cook, turning, until golden brown on all four sides but tuna is still pink in the middle, about 30 seconds per side. Let cool before slicing crosswise ¼ inch thick.

2. Dollop ¼ teaspoon mayonnaise onto center of each cracker. Top with a slice of tuna, and brush fish with sesame oil; top with ¼ teaspoon roe and sprinkle with sesame seeds.

ROASTED WILD MUSHROOMS AND GOAT CHEESE ON RYE TRIANGLES
makes 24

■

- 12 ounces assorted wild mushrooms, such as oyster, hen-of-the woods, and shiitake
- 2 tablespoons extra-virgin olive oil

  Coarse salt and freshly ground pepper
- 12 slices party-size rye bread, cut in half to make 24 triangles
- 8 ounces fresh goat cheese, room temperature

  Small fresh flat-leaf parsley leaves, for garnish

1. Preheat oven to 375°F. On a rimmed baking sheet, toss mushrooms with oil; season with salt and pepper. Spread in a single layer, and roast, tossing once or twice, until browned, 12 to 14 minutes. Let cool.

2. Dividing evenly, top each bread triangle with a dollop of goat cheese, then mushrooms. Sprinkle with pepper, and garnish with parsley.

SMOKED TROUT, CRÈME FRAÎCHE, AND PICKLED ONIONS ON PUMPERNICKEL
makes 24

■

- ½ cup crème fraîche
- 12 slices party-size pumpernickel bread, cut in half to make 24 rectangles
- 6 ounces smoked trout, flaked
- ½ cup very thinly sliced pickled onions (see note, right)

Dollop 1 teaspoon crème fraîche onto each bread rectangle, then top with smoked trout and pickled onions, dividing evenly.

BLACK-OLIVE BUTTER AND RADISHES ON BAGUETTE
makes 64

■

- 1 to 2 ficelles or thin baguettes, cut into 64 thin rounds

  Extra-virgin olive oil, for brushing
- ½ cup pitted oil-cured black olives, finely chopped
- 2 scallions, trimmed and finely chopped
- 3 tablespoons finely chopped fresh mint leaves
- ½ cup (1 stick) unsalted butter, room temperature

  Freshly ground pepper
- 1 bunch radishes, very thinly sliced

Preheat oven to 350°F. Brush bread with oil, then toast on a baking sheet until just turning crisp, 8 to 10 minutes. Let cool completely. In a bowl, mix together olives, scallions, mint, and butter. Season with pepper. Spread olive-butter mixture onto toasts, dividing evenly. Top each with a radish slice.

NOTE You can use pickled onions from a jar or make your own: In a skillet, heat 1 teaspoon extra-virgin olive oil over medium. Add 1 red onion, thinly sliced, and cook 1 minute. Add 2 teaspoons sugar, and cook, stirring, until dissolved. Stir in 2 tablespoons red-wine vinegar, and season with coarse salt. Transfer to a bowl, and let cool completely before using. Pickled onions can be refrigerated, covered, up to 1 week.

This one-bite version of Italian rollatine involves little time or effort, and just a few ingredients. Grilled eggplant slices become tender wrappers for crumbled feta and toasted pine nuts; a single basil leaf garnishes each roll. They pair perfectly with the Roasted Polenta Squares with Fontina and Wild Mushrooms (page 207) and a medium-bodied Italian wine such as Chianti or Nero d'Avola.

Grilled Eggplant with Feta, Basil, and Pine Nuts

—

makes about 20

1 pound Japanese eggplants (about 2)

Extra-virgin olive oil, for brushing

Coarse salt and freshly ground pepper

¼ cup plus 2 tablespoons crumbled feta cheese (3 ounces)

¼ cup pine nuts, lightly toasted (see page 242)

Fresh basil leaves, for garnish

1. Heat a grill (or grill pan) to medium-high. (If using a charcoal grill, coals are ready when you can hold the palm of your hand 6 inches above grates for just 3 to 4 seconds.) Trim ends of eggplants, and cut lengthwise into ¼-inch-thick slices. Brush both sides with oil, and season generously with salt and pepper. Brush grates with oil. Grill, turning once, until soft and lightly charred in places, 2 to 3 minutes per side. Let cool completely.

2. Cut each eggplant slice in half crosswise. Divide feta and pine nuts evenly among slices, placing them on one end of each, and gently pressing pine nuts into cheese to adhere. Roll up eggplant, and secure with a cocktail skewer or toothpick. Tuck a basil leaf into top of each and serve.

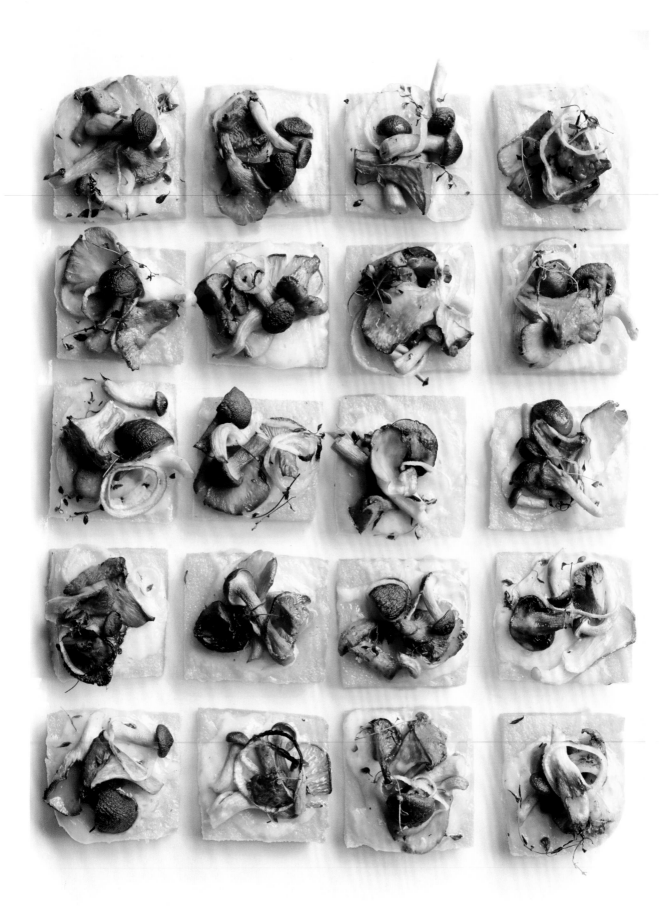

Comfort food, meet finger food: Little squares of polenta are topped with cheese and wild mushrooms, then roasted until crisp, golden, and delicious. Here, a mix of mushrooms gives the best range of textures and earthy flavors, and the assortment also looks more interesting than just one variety of mushroom would.

Roasted Polenta Squares with Fontina and Wild Mushrooms

makes 24

Coarse salt

1½ cups coarse-ground polenta

8 ounces mixed mushrooms, such as cremini, oyster, chanterelle, and hen-of-the-woods, trimmed and thinly sliced

1 shallot, thinly sliced

1 teaspoon fresh thyme leaves

3 tablespoons extra-virgin olive oil, plus more for brushing

1½ cups shredded Italian fontina cheese

MAKE AHEAD Once polenta is cold and set, it can be covered with plastic wrap and refrigerated up to 3 days.

1. Bring 4½ cups water to a boil in a large, heavy-bottomed pot, then add salt. Bring another 4 cups water to a simmer in a small saucepan. Gradually add polenta to the large pot, whisking constantly until combined. Reduce heat until only one or two large bubbles break the surface at a time, adjusting heat as necessary.

2. Whisk 2 ladles of simmering water into polenta, and cook, stirring frequently with a wooden spoon, until water has been absorbed, about 5 minutes. Continue to add 2 ladlefuls of water every 5 minutes, stirring often and waiting for it to be absorbed before adding more, until polenta is creamy and just pulls away from sides of pot, about 45 minutes. (Adjust heat as necessary.)

3. Pour polenta into a slightly damp 9-by-13-inch baking dish. Let stand until no longer steaming, about 10 minutes. Refrigerate, uncovered, until cold and set, about 1½ hours.

4. Preheat oven to 450°F. In a bowl, toss together mushrooms, shallot, thyme, and oil; season with salt.

5. Turn out polenta onto a cutting board. Cut into 24 pieces, and transfer to a rimmed baking sheet brushed with oil. Dividing evenly, brush tops with oil, then sprinkle with cheese and top with mushroom mixture. Roast until polenta is crisp on bottom, cheese is melted, and mushrooms are wilted and golden brown, about 25 minutes. Serve immediately.

A selection of ceviches makes for a light and refreshing buffet. The ones shown here offer a variety of seafood and a range of bright flavors, and each type is served in its own vessel. From left to right: Shrimp with avocado in toasted corn cups; red snapper and citrus in lettuce cups or baby peppers; and scallops and watermelon in Japanese soup spoons.

Ceviches

Ceviches

SHRIMP WITH AVOCADO
makes about 20 hors d'oeuvres

—

1 pound medium shell-on shrimp (30 to 40 count)

1 teaspoon coarse salt, plus more if needed

½ teaspoon sugar, plus more if needed

2 tablespoons extra-virgin olive oil

1 navel orange, peel and pith removed, cut into segments and chopped

½ small pink grapefruit, peel and pith removed, cut into segments and chopped

1 jalapeño chile, thinly sliced (ribs and seeds removed for less heat, if desired)

1 ripe but firm avocado, pitted, peeled, and diced

¼ cup coarsely chopped fresh cilantro leaves

Toasted Corn Cups (recipe follows)

1. Bring a pot of water to a boil and add shrimp. Cover, turn off heat, and let shrimp cook until pink and opaque throughout, about 2 minutes. Transfer to an ice-water bath and let cool. Peel, devein, and cut shrimp in half lengthwise.

2. Transfer shrimp to a large nonreactive bowl, and add salt, sugar, and oil. Gently fold in orange and grapefruit segments, jalapeño, avocado, and cilantro. Season with a pinch more salt or sugar if necessary. Divide evenly among corn cups and serve.

Toasted Corn Cups
makes 24

—

12 corn tortillas (6 inch)

Safflower oil, for brushing

1. Preheat oven to 350°F. Use a 2¾-inch round cookie cutter to cut out 2 rounds from each tortilla for a total of 24 rounds. Working in batches, place tortillas in a steamer basket (or colander) set in a pan filled with 2 inches of water; bring to a boil, then reduce to a simmer. Cover and steam until tortillas are slightly softened and warm. Quickly transfer to a baking sheet, and brush both sides with oil.

2. Press rounds into a 24-cup mini-muffin tin. Bake until tortillas are crisp and just beginning to brown, about 20 minutes. Remove from heat; transfer cups to a wire rack to cool completely.

MAKE AHEAD Corn cups may be made several days ahead and kept in an airtight container at room temperature or frozen for up to 3 weeks. To reheat from frozen, arrange in a single layer on a baking sheet and warm in a 250°F oven, about 5 minutes.

SNAPPER AND SQUID
makes about 20 hors d'oeuvres

—

2 limes

1 navel orange

8 ounces red snapper fillet, skin removed, finely chopped

¼ pound small shell-on shrimp (40 to 50 count), peeled and deveined (see page 242)

¼ pound cleaned squid, thinly sliced into rings

½ red onion, finely chopped

3 tomatoes (about 1 pound)

¼ cup packed fresh cilantro leaves, finely chopped

1 teaspoon hot sauce, or to taste

Coarse salt

20 baby bell peppers, halved, ribs and seeds removed, or 20 baby romaine lettuce leaves

1. Grate 1 teaspoon zest each from 1 lime and the orange into a bowl. Squeeze juice from limes and orange into separate bowls. In a large nonreactive bowl, combine seafood, zests, half the lime juice, and all the orange juice; toss to combine. Cover and refrigerate at least 1 hour or up to 12 hours.

2. Meanwhile, soak onion in a bowl of cold water 10 minutes; drain well.

3. Peel tomatoes (see page 242); cut into quarters. Working over a sieve set in a bowl, remove pulp and seeds from tomato quarters. Mash pulp and seeds with back of a spoon to extract as much tomato water as possible. Discard solids left in sieve. Finely chop tomato quarters.

4. Add onion, chopped tomato and tomato water, cilantro, hot sauce, and remaining lime juice to seafood, stirring gently to combine. Cover and marinate in refrigerator 1 hour. Season with salt just before serving, dividing evenly among pepper halves or lettuce leaves.

SCALLOP WITH WATERMELON
makes about 20 hors d'oeuvres

—

1 pound small bay scallops

¾ cup fresh lime juice (from 6 to 7 limes), plus more for serving

1 teaspoon coarse salt

2 jalapeño chiles, minced (ribs and seeds removed for less heat, if desired)

1 cup finely chopped seedless watermelon

1. Place scallops in a large nonreactive bowl. Add lime juice and salt; toss well. Cover; refrigerate 30 minutes. Drain, discarding liquid. Refrigerate scallops until ready to use, up to 2 hours.

2. To serve, place a scallop in each Japanese soup spoon, add diced watermelon and jalapeño, and sprinkle with more lime juice.

Partygoers have been enjoying stuffed mushrooms for decades, and with good reason. The gentle round of the button mushroom cap is tailor-made for filling, here in an updated tasty selection of herbed sweet sausage, kale and fontina cheese, and red bell pepper and goat cheese. After baking the mushrooms, serve them right away, when they're at their very best—moist and tender, and golden on top.

Stuffed Mushrooms

SAUSAGE AND HERBS
makes 24

—

1 tablespoon extra-virgin olive oil, plus more for drizzling

6 ounces sweet Italian sausage (about 2 links), removed from casings

2 garlic cloves, minced

1 large shallot, minced

24 large button mushrooms, caps cleaned, stems removed and finely chopped

Coarse salt and freshly ground pepper

1 tablespoon finely chopped fresh flat-leaf parsley leaves

2 teaspoons finely chopped fresh oregano leaves, plus whole leaves for garnish (optional)

1 large egg, lightly beaten

2 tablespoons plain dry breadcrumbs (see page 242)

2 tablespoons finely grated Parmigiano-Reggiano cheese

1. Preheat oven to 375°F. In a large skillet, heat oil over medium-high. Cook sausage, breaking it up with a fork, until no longer pink, about 5 minutes. Add garlic, shallot, and chopped mushroom stems; season with salt and pepper. Reduce heat to medium, and cook until vegetables are tender, stirring occasionally, 4 to 6 minutes. Transfer to a bowl, stir in parsley and oregano, and let cool.

2. Add egg, breadcrumbs, and cheese to cooled sausage mixture; stir to combine. Place mushroom caps on a rimmed baking sheet. Season cavities with salt and pepper, then stuff with sausage mixture, dividing evenly and packing tightly. Drizzle lightly with oil.

3. Bake until mushrooms are tender and tops are browned, 25 to 30 minutes. Serve immediately, garnished with additional oregano leaves, if desired.

MAKE AHEAD Arrange baked and cooled stuffed mushroom caps on a rimmed baking sheet in a single layer. Freeze until firm, about 1 hour. Transfer to a resealable plastic bag, and freeze up to 3 months. Reheat (without thawing) on a parchment-lined baking sheet in a 375°F oven, about 10 minutes.

Fillings for Stuffed Mushrooms

KALE AND FONTINA
makes 24

—

1 small bunch kale (12 ounces)

1 tablespoon unsalted butter

2 tablespoons minced shallot

1 tablespoon all-purpose flour

1 cup milk

Pinch of cayenne pepper

24 large button mushrooms, stems removed and caps cleaned

Coarse salt

½ cup grated Italian fontina or Taleggio cheese

1. Preheat oven to 375°F. Place kale in a steamer basket (or colander) set in a saucepan filled with 2 inches of water; bring to a boil, then reduce to a simmer. Cover and steam until kale is tender, about 10 minutes. Transfer kale to a sieve to drain, then squeeze out as much liquid as possible.

2. Melt butter in a small saucepan over medium-high heat. Add shallot and cook, stirring, until softened, about 2 minutes. Add flour and cook, stirring, 1 minute. Add milk, whisking until mixture just comes to a simmer. Gently simmer, stirring, until mixture is thickened, 5 to 7 minutes. Stir in kale, and season with salt and cayenne pepper.

3. Place mushroom caps on a rimmed baking sheet. Season cavities with salt, then stuff with kale mixture, dividing evenly and packing tightly. Top with cheese.

4. Bake until mushrooms are tender and cheese is melted and golden, 25 to 30 minutes. Serve immediately.

GOAT CHEESE AND RED BELL PEPPER
makes 24

———

2 slices day-old white bread, crusts removed

1 scallion, white and pale-green parts only, coarsely chopped

½ red bell pepper, ribs and seeds removed, coarsely chopped

2 ounces fresh goat cheese

2 tablespoons finely chopped fresh cilantro leaves

¼ cup grated Monterey Jack cheese or Parmigiano-Reggiano cheese

Coarse salt and freshly ground black pepper

24 large button mushrooms, stems removed and caps cleaned

1. Pulse bread in a food processor until finely chopped. Transfer to a bowl. Combine scallion, bell pepper, and goat cheese in food processor, and pulse until finely chopped and well combined. Transfer mixture to bowl with breadcrumbs, and stir to combine. Stir in cilantro and half the grated Monterey Jack; season with salt and pepper.

2. Preheat oven to 375°F. Place mushroom caps on a rimmed baking sheet. Season cavities with salt and pepper, then stuff with goat cheese mixture, dividing evenly and packing tightly.

3. Bake until mushrooms are tender, 25 to 30 minutes. Turn oven to broil. Sprinkle mushrooms with remaining grated cheese, and broil until cheese is golden, about 1 minute. Serve immediately.

With its outstanding flavor, jumbo lump crabmeat is the best choice for crab cakes. A variety of toppings lets guests choose from a spike of Asian flavor (wasabi mayonnaise), a traditional tartar sauce infused with tarragon, or mashed avocado with lime.

Mini Crab Cakes

makes about 34

¼ cup plain fresh breadcrumbs (see page 242)

1 pound lump crabmeat, picked over

1 large egg

3 tablespoons mayonnaise

2 teaspoons fresh lemon juice

Dash of hot sauce (such as Tabasco)

Coarse salt and freshly ground pepper

Yellow medium-ground cornmeal, for sprinkling

3 tablespoons safflower oil

Toppings (recipes follow)

1. In a large bowl, gently mix together bread-crumbs, crabmeat, egg, mayonnaise, lemon juice, and hot sauce. Season with salt and pepper. (The mixture will be wet.) Form into 1-inch-diameter patties. Sprinkle a rimmed baking sheet with cornmeal, then place patties on sheet and sprinkle tops with cornmeal. Freeze until firm, at least 1 hour.

2. Preheat oven to 200°F. Heat oil in a large nonstick skillet over medium until hot but not smoking. Working in batches, fry crab cakes until golden brown and warmed through, 2 to 3 minutes per side. Transfer to a paper-towel-lined baking sheet, and keep warm in the oven while finishing batches. Serve with desired toppings.

Toppings

TARRAGON TARTAR SAUCE
Stir together ⅓ cup **mayonnaise**, 1 tablespoon **sweet relish**, 1 teaspoon fresh **lemon** juice, 1 tablespoon chopped **capers** (drained and rinsed), and 1 teaspoon chopped **fresh tarragon** leaves; season with **coarse salt** and freshly ground **pepper**. Sauce can be refrigerated, covered, up to 1 week. Garnish with more capers.

MASHED AVOCADO
Mash 1 ripe but firm pitted and peeled **avocado** until smooth. Stir in juice of ½ **lime** and season with **coarse salt**.

WASABI MAYONNAISE
Stir together ½ cup **mayonnaise** and 1 table-spoon plus 1½ teaspoons **wasabi paste**.

MAKE AHEAD Crab cakes can be prepared through step 1 and frozen up to 1 week; once firm, transfer to resealable plastic bags. Thaw overnight in the refrigerator before frying as directed.

Brightly colored soups offer a good dose of festivity and are perfect for serving in handheld sippable portions, either cold or at room temperature. The bonus: no spoons required, just petite vessels, like these votive holders. Our pureed vegetable-based soups (shown opposite, top row, from left to right)—beet, butternut squash, spinach and pea, and yellow tomato and mango—pack a lot of flavor in small doses and help to balance any heavier hors d'oeuvres on the menu.

Pureed Vegetable Soups

YELLOW TOMATO AND MANGO GAZPACHO
makes 32 (2-ounce) shots

3 pounds large yellow tomatoes, peeled (see page 242), cored, and quartered

2 mangoes, peeled, pitted, and chopped (see page 242)

1 yellow bell pepper, ribs and seeds removed, chopped

1 jalapeño chile, chopped (ribs and seeds removed if less heat is desired)

2 garlic cloves, smashed

1 tablespoon plus 1 teaspoon champagne vinegar

2 tablespoons extra-virgin olive oil

Coarse salt

1. Working in batches, puree tomatoes with mangoes, bell pepper, jalapeño, garlic, vinegar, oil, and 2 cups water in a blender or food processor. Season with salt. Strain through a fine sieve into a bowl, pressing on solids to remove as much liquid as possible. Refrigerate, covered, until cold, at least 4 hours or up to 1 day.

2. Before serving, whisk soup until smooth and creamy, adding up to ½ cup cold water if necessary to reach desired consistency. Divide evenly among 32 cups. Serve cold.

Pureed Vegetable Soups

BEET SOUP
makes 24 (2-ounce) shots

—

2 pounds red beets
2 tablespoons extra-virgin olive oil
1 onion, chopped
  Coarse salt and freshly ground pepper
1¾ cups low-sodium chicken broth
1 to 2 teaspoons fresh lemon juice
  (to taste)

1. Peel beets with a sharp knife, then coarsely chop. In a large pot, heat oil over medium. Add onion and season with salt. Cook, stirring occasionally, until softened, 5 to 7 minutes. Add beets, chicken broth, and enough water to cover (4 to 5 cups). Bring to a boil, then reduce heat and simmer until beets are easily pierced with the tip of a paring knife, 20 to 25 minutes. Let cool slightly.

2. Working in batches (do not fill jar more than halfway), puree beet mixture in a blender until smooth. Stir in enough water (up to 3 tablespoons) to reach desired consistency. Season with salt, pepper, and lemon juice. Divide among 24 cups. Serve at room temperature.

MAKE AHEAD Beet soup can be prepared up to 3 days ahead; let cool completely before refrigerating, covered. Bring to room temperature before serving.

BUTTERNUT SQUASH SOUP
makes 32 (2-ounce) shots

—

3 pounds butternut squash
2 tablespoons extra-virgin olive oil
1 onion, chopped
  Coarse salt and freshly ground pepper
1¾ cups low-sodium chicken broth
1 to 2 teaspoons fresh lemon juice
  (to taste)

1. Peel butternut squash; halve lengthwise, remove seeds, and cut into 1-inch pieces. In a large pot, heat oil over medium. Add onion and season with salt. Cook, stirring occasionally, until softened, 5 to 7 minutes.

2. Add squash, chicken broth, and enough water to cover (4 to 5 cups). Bring to a boil, then reduce heat and simmer until squash is easily pierced with the tip of a paring knife, about 20 minutes. Let cool slightly.

3. Working in batches (do not fill jar more than halfway), puree squash mixture in a blender until smooth. Stir in enough water (up to 3 tablespoons) to reach desired consistency. Season with salt, pepper, and lemon juice. Divide among 32 cups. Serve at room temperature.

MAKE AHEAD Squash soup can be prepared up to 3 days ahead; let cool completely before refrigerating, covered. Bring to room temperature before serving.

CHILLED SPINACH-PEA SOUP
makes 24 (2-ounce) shots

■

- 3 tablespoons unsalted butter
- 5 leeks, white and pale-green parts only, cut into ¼-inch-thick slices, washed well and drained
  Coarse salt and freshly ground pepper
- 1 pound spinach, tough stems trimmed
- 3 cups low-sodium chicken broth
- ¾ cup fresh tarragon leaves
- 15 ounces thawed frozen peas

1. Melt butter in a medium skillet over medium. Add leeks; cook, stirring occasionally, until softened, about 10 minutes. Season with salt and pepper. Add spinach and cook just until wilted, tossing occasionally, 2 to 3 minutes.

2. Stir in chicken broth, and simmer until spinach is tender but still bright green, about 6 minutes. Stir in tarragon and peas, and cook, stirring occasionally, 5 minutes.

3. Working in batches (do not fill jar more than halfway), puree leek mixture in a blender until smooth. Strain through a sieve into a bowl, pressing on solids to remove as much liquid as possible. Refrigerate until cold, at least 4 hours or up to 3 days.

4. Before serving, whisk soup until smooth and creamy. Divide among 24 cups. Serve cold.

MAKE AHEAD Spinach-pea soup can be prepared up to 3 days ahead; let cool completely before refrigerating, covered.

GARNISHES

Although the soups pictured on page 219 are served without garnishes, they could each be embellished with something crisp or creamy on top. Here are some of our favorite finishing touches.

Fried Leeks

Cut leek (white and pale-green parts only) into fine julienne and wash well; dry thoroughly on paper towels. Heat 2½ inches of safflower oil in a small pot over medium-high until it reaches 300°F on a deep-fry thermometer. Working in batches (if necessary), fry leek until golden and crisp, 1 to 3 minutes. Use a slotted spoon to transfer to paper towels to drain; let cool completely. Refrigerate in an airtight container up to 2 days; serve at room temperature.

Herbed Croutons

Preheat oven to 350°F. Trim crusts and cut white sandwich bread into ¼-inch cubes. Toss bread with 1 tablespoon melted unsalted butter on a rimmed baking sheet. Toast in oven, tossing once, until pale golden, 9 to 10 minutes. Store in an airtight container at room temperature up to 3 days. Toss with a tablespoon of chopped fresh herbs, such as flat-leaf parsley, basil, or marjoram, before using.

Lardons

Cut thick-cut bacon slices into ¼-inch dice. Fry in a skillet over medium heat until fat has rendered and bacon is crisp, about 8 minutes. Use a slotted spoon or spatula to transfer to paper towels to drain and cool before using.

Prosciutto Crisps

Preheat oven to 400°F. Cut thinly sliced prosciutto into small strips. Arrange in a single layer on a rimmed baking sheet. Bake until crisp, about 10 minutes. Transfer to paper towels to drain; let cool completely. Store in an airtight container, between sheets of parchment, at room temperature up to 2 days.

Herbed Crème Fraîche

Pulse ½ cup crème fraîche, 2 tablespoons chopped fresh herbs, such as basil, flat-leaf parsley, or mint, and ¼ teaspoon each coarse salt and freshly ground pepper in a food processor until thoroughly combined. Refrigerate, covered, up to 2 days.

Roasted Pepitas

Preheat oven to 375°F. On a rimmed baking sheet, toss pepitas with extra-virgin olive oil, coarse salt and freshly ground black pepper, and a pinch or two of cayenne pepper or cumin or ground cardamom. Spread in a single layer and roast until completely dried and crisp, tossing occasionally, about 15 minutes. Let cool completely. Store in an airtight container at room temperature up to 3 days.

A lunchtime and teatime tradition, chicken salad joins the party when tucked into easy tartlet shells made from buttered bread and shaped in mini-muffin cups. We've included three versions: a classic chicken salad with celery and tarragon; another with dried apricots and chives; and a curried salad with the sweet-tart crunch of diced Granny Smith apples.

Chicken-Salad Tartlets

CLASSIC CHICKEN SALAD
makes enough for 48 tartlets

—

- 1 quart low-sodium chicken broth
- 1 pound boneless, skinless chicken breast halves
- ½ cup diced celery (from 2 to 3 stalks)
- ½ cup mayonnaise
- Juice of 1 lemon
- 1 tablespoon finely chopped fresh tarragon leaves, plus whole small leaves for garnish
- Coarse salt and freshly ground pepper
- Tartlet Shells (recipe follows)

1. Bring broth to a boil in a large saucepan. Add chicken, reduce heat, and simmer until cooked through, about 15 minutes. Drain, reserving broth for another use, and let chicken cool. Shred into bite-size pieces.

2. In a bowl, combine chicken, celery, mayonnaise, lemon juice, and tarragon; season with salt and pepper, and mix to combine. Divide among shells (about 1 tablespoon in each); garnish with whole tarragon leaves.

Tartlet Shells
makes 48

—

- 12 slices white sandwich bread
- 4 tablespoons unsalted butter, melted

Preheat oven to 375°F. With a rolling pin, roll out bread slices ⅛ inch thick. Remove crusts and cut each slice into four 2-inch squares. Brush both sides with melted butter; press into mini-muffin cups. Bake until golden brown, about 10 minutes. Remove from tins; let cool before filling, as desired.

MAKE AHEAD The tartlet shells can be baked up to a day ahead; store in an airtight container at room temperature.

Fillings for Tartlets

CHICKEN SALAD WITH APRICOTS AND CHIVES
makes enough for 48 tartlets

—

- 1 quart low-sodium chicken broth
- 1 pound boneless, skinless chicken breast halves
- ⅔ cup plain Greek yogurt
- 2½ teaspoons Dijon mustard
- 2 tablespoons minced fresh chives
- ¼ cup chopped toasted almonds (see page 242)
- ¼ cup chopped dried apricots
- Coarse salt and freshly ground pepper
- Tartlet Shells (page 223)

1. Bring broth to a boil in a large saucepan. Add chicken, reduce heat, and simmer just until cooked through, about 15 minutes. Drain, reserving broth for another use, and let chicken cool. Cut into bite-size pieces.

2. In a bowl, combine yogurt, mustard, chives, almonds, and apricots. Stir in chicken and season with salt and pepper. Mix to combine. Divide among shells.

CURRIED CHICKEN SALAD
makes enough for 48 tartlets

—

- 1 quart low-sodium chicken broth
- 1 pound boneless, skinless chicken breast halves
- ⅓ cup plain Greek yogurt
- ⅓ cup mayonnaise
- 1½ teaspoons curry powder
- 1 tablespoon thinly sliced scallions
- ½ Granny Smith apple, cored and cut into ½-inch pieces
- Coarse salt and freshly ground pepper
- Sliced almonds, toasted (see page 242), for garnish
- Tartlet Shells (page 223)

1. Bring broth to a boil in a large saucepan. Add chicken, reduce heat, and simmer just until cooked through, about 15 minutes. Drain, reserving broth for another use, and let chicken cool. Cut into bite-size pieces.

2. In a bowl, combine yogurt, mayonnaise, curry powder, scallions, and apple; season with salt and pepper. Stir in chicken. Divide among shells; garnish each with an almond slice.

Tiny, yes, but big on personality: In this playful spin on the BLT, all the makings of the sandwich (minus the bread) are combined in a single bite. Colorful cherry tomatoes are topped with a dollop of mayonnaise, lettuce tendrils, and tiny bits of bacon.

Cherry Tomato BLTs
—

makes 48

48 cherry tomatoes (about
    1 quart)

⅓ cup mayonnaise

6 slices bacon, cooked until
   crisp, drained, and finely
   chopped

   Coarse salt and freshly
   ground pepper

1 cup very finely shredded
   iceberg lettuce

1. Trim bottom of tomatoes flat so they stand upright. Use a serrated knife to slice off top ¼ inch. Scoop out seeds and pulp and place tomato shells, upside down, on a paper-towel-lined baking sheet to drain.

2. Place mayonnaise in a small resealable plastic bag, and snip one corner. Flip tomatoes upright, and squeeze a pea-size dollop of mayonnaise into bottom of each. Sprinkle half of bacon evenly among tomatoes, then season with salt and pepper. Stuff tomatoes with lettuce, sprinkle with remaining bacon, and dab with more mayonnaise. Serve immediately or refrigerate in an airtight container up to 3 hours.

Some holiday foods deserve to be enjoyed beyond the ceremonial feast. Latkes, a Hanukkah tradition, are versatile enough to be paired with a range of toppings—some savory, some sweet, some traditional (sour cream, salmon roe, and chives), some not (Nova lox and Meyer lemon). They are also a fantastic make-ahead option: Fry them up to a month ahead, then freeze and reheat in the oven before serving.

Latkes

—

makes about 40

4 large russet potatoes, peeled

½ white onion, grated

2 large eggs, lightly beaten

¼ cup beer, such as lager

3 tablespoons all-purpose flour

1 tablespoon coarse salt

1 teapoon freshly ground pepper

   Safflower oil, for frying

1. Using the julienne attachment of an adjustable-blade slicer or the small holes of a box grater, grate potatoes in long strips into a bowl of cold water. Use a slotted spoon to transfer potatoes to another bowl, reserving liquid in large bowl.

2. Let reserved liquid stand 10 minutes to allow starch to sink to bottom of bowl (see note below). Carefully pour off liquid from bowl, reserving milky residue (potato starch). Transfer potatoes back to bowl with the starch. Add onion. Stir in eggs, beer, flour, salt, and pepper.

3. Preheat oven to 200°F. Line a baking sheet with paper towels. Heat ½ inch oil in a large skillet. Working in batches, add ¼ cup potato mixture per latke. Cook until golden brown, 2 to 3 minutes per side. Transfer to baking sheet; keep warm in the oven. Serve with desired toppings.

Toppings

CRANBERRY-APPLE CHUTNEY
In a saucepan, bring 1 bag (12 ounces) **cranberries**, 1 chopped **Granny Smith apple**, ¾ cup **sugar**, 1 teaspoon finely grated **lemon** zest, and 1 cup **water** to a boil; reduce heat and simmer until berries are soft and bursting, about 10 minutes. Let cool.

CUCUMBER AND GREEK YOGURT
Stir ¼ cup diced **English cucumber** into ½ cup plain **Greek yogurt**; dollop mixture on latkes and top with small **dill** sprigs.

APPLE AND BLUE CHEESE
Top each latke with 1 thin **lady-apple slice** (cut crosswise) and crumbled mild **blue cheese**.

LOX AND MEYER LEMON
Top each latke with 1 thin slice **Nova lox**, folded over to fit, and 1 very thin slice **Meyer lemon**.

SOUR CREAM AND ROE
Dollop latke with **sour cream**, top with **salmon roe**, and sprinkle with snipped **fresh chives**.

MAKE AHEAD Fried latkes can be cooled, then frozen in a single layer on a baking sheet until firm, about 1 hour; transfer to resealable plastic bags, and freeze up to 1 month. Reheat without thawing on a parchment-lined baking sheet in a 350°F oven, about 15 minutes.

NOTE The natural starches from the potatoes that leach out in the reserved liquid are used to bind the potato mixture. Test by cooking one latke; if it doesn't hold together, add 1 to 2 tablespoons potato starch to the batter before cooking the rest.

Make way for little squares of heaven—these fried morsels are sure to be voted most popular at any party. You can (and should) prepare the stovetop macaroni and cheese a few days ahead, since it will firm up in the refrigerator, for easier cutting. Then follow a two-step breading process, using panko instead of regular breadcrumbs for a crust that's crisp yet light. Don't be put off by the yield; the squares fry quickly, in three or four batches, and you can reheat replenishments over the course of the evening—whenever the platter is wiped clean (which will be often).

Fried Macaroni-and-Cheese Bites
—

makes about 10 dozen

Coarse salt

1 pound elbow macaroni

5 tablespoons unsalted butter

¼ cup plus 2 tablespoons all-purpose flour

4 cups milk, room temperature

¾ teaspoon mustard powder

4¾ cups grated white cheddar cheese (about 14 ounces), room temperature

½ to ¾ cup safflower oil, for frying, plus more for parchment

4 large eggs

2 cups panko

MAKE AHEAD The recipe can be prepared through step 3 up to 3 days ahead.

Once fried, the squares can rest on a baking sheet lined with a wire rack up to 1 hour; reheat in a 350°F oven (on the rack and sheet), about 5 minutes.

1. In a large pot of boiling salted water, cook macaroni until al dente according to package instructions; drain.

2. In pot, melt 4 tablespoons butter over medium heat. Whisk in flour, and cook, stirring frequently, until mixture is pale golden and has a nutty aroma, about 4 minutes. Whisking constantly, slowly add milk. Cook, whisking along bottom of pot, until boiling, about 7 minutes. Reduce heat and gently simmer, stirring occasionally, until sauce is thickened, 10 to 12 minutes. Remove from heat, and add remaining 1 tablespoon butter and the cheese. Stir until melted and sauce is smooth; season with salt. Add macaroni to sauce, and stir to combine.

3. Line a 9-by-13-inch baking dish with parchment; brush parchment lightly with oil. Spread macaroni mixture evenly in dish. Cover and refrigerate until firm, at least 8 hours.

4. Invert set macaroni and cheese onto a cutting board and remove parchment. Cut into 1-inch squares with a sharp knife.

5. Whisk eggs in a shallow dish. Combine panko and cayenne in another shallow dish, and season with salt. Dip macaroni squares, a few at a time, in eggs, allowing excess to drip off into dish, then roll in panko mixture to coat completely. Transfer to a wire rack set on a baking sheet.

6. Heat 2 tablespoons oil in a large nonstick skillet over medium until shimmering. Working in batches, add coated squares in a single layer (do not crowd pan); cook, turning occasionally, until all sides are crisp and golden brown, 5 to 7 minutes total. Transfer to a paper-towel-lined rack to drain and cool slightly. Wipe skillet clean. Repeat process with more oil and remaining squares. Serve warm.

Garlic bread, Spanish-style: Rub baguette slices with garlic cloves, brush with extra-virgin olive oil, and grill to a crisp, then rub with cut plum tomatoes—that's the traditional version of these Catalan toasts. Here, they're given the special-occasion treatment with oven-dried tomatoes, fresh herbs, and other toppings, all inspired by the flavors of the region.

Pan Tomate

—

makes about 24

8 small ripe plum tomatoes, 6 cored and cut into ¼-inch-thick slices lengthwise, 2 halved and seeded

2 teaspoons fresh thyme leaves

3 tablespoons fresh marjoram leaves, chopped

¼ cup extra-virgin olive oil, plus more for grill

Coarse salt and freshly ground pepper

1 baguette, cut into ¼-inch-thick slices on the bias

4 garlic cloves, halved

Assorted toppings, such as anchovies, Serrano ham, marinated artichoke-heart quarters (page 119), or sliced hard-boiled eggs (see note, below)

1. Preheat oven to 250°F. Toss tomato slices with thyme, 1 tablespoon marjoram, and 2 tablespoons oil. Season with salt and pepper. Arrange tomato slices in a single layer on a parchment-lined rimmed baking sheet. Bake 1 hour.

2. Reduce oven temperature to 200°F. Continue baking until tomatoes are shriveled, about 2 hours more.

3. Heat a grill (or grill pan) to medium-high. (If using a charcoal grill, coals are ready when you can hold the palm of your hand 6 inches above grates for just 3 to 4 seconds.) Brush grates with oil. Rub baguette slices with garlic. Brush lightly with remaining 2 tablespoons oil, dividing evenly. Grill baguette slices until crisp, about 1 minute per side. Rub with reserved plum tomato halves. Divide dried tomato slices evenly among toasts, then add toppings as desired. Garnish with remaining 2 tablespoons marjoram.

MAKE AHEAD Oven-dried tomatoes can be refrigerated in an airtight container up to 1 week. Bring to room temperature before using.

NOTE See page 180 for how to make perfect hard-boiled eggs. For topping these treats, use center slices, with the yolk (save the ends for another use).

Sips

Tumblers

SIDECAR
makes 1

Fill glass with ice. Add 1 ounce (2 tablespoons) **Cognac**, 1 ounce (2 tablespoons) **calvados**, and 1 teaspoon fresh **lemon** juice. Stir to combine. Drop in a thin strip of **red-apple** peel and serve.

RAMOS GIN FIZZ
makes 1

In a cocktail shaker filled with ice, combine 1 ounce (2 tablespoons) **gin**, 3 dashes fresh **lime** juice, 3 dashes fresh **lemon** juice, 3 dashes **orange-flower water**, 2 teaspoons **superfine sugar**, 1 large **egg white**, and ¼ cup **light cream**. Shake vigorously; pour into glass. Top with ¼ cup **seltzer**; garnish with ground cinnamon, if desired, and serve.

LEMON OUZO-ADE
makes 6

Heat 1 cup **sugar**, 1 cup water, and 12 strips **lemon** zest in a saucepan over high heat, stirring occasionally, until sugar dissolves. Let simple syrup cool. In a pitcher, stir ¾ cup syrup (refrigerate remaining up to 1 month), 6 ounces (¾ cup) chilled **ouzo**, ½ cup plus 1 tablespoon fresh **lemon juice**, and ice. Divide among ice-filled glasses; serve.

GINGER CAIPIRINHA
makes 1

Place 2 thin slices peeled **fresh ginger** and 1 tablespoon **sugar** in a glass; mash ginger with a muddler or wooden spoon. Add a quartered **lime**; crush with muddler. Fill with crushed ice; add 2 ounces (¼ cup) **cachaça**. Stir. Garnish with a lime wedge; serve.

GIN-AND-GRAPEFRUIT FIZZES
makes 8

In a pitcher, mash ½ thinly sliced **English cucumber** with a muddler or wooden spoon. Add 12 ounces (1½ cups) **gin**. Chill 12 hours and up to 3 days. Fill glass with ice. Pour 1½ ounces (3 tablespoons) cucumber-gin into each; top with **grapefruit soda**. Stir, garnish with cucumber slices, and serve.

TEQUILA-THYME LEMONADE
makes 1

In a glass, muddle 3 **thyme** sprigs with 1 teaspoon **superfine sugar** and 2 **lemon** wedges. Add 3 ounces (¼ cup plus 2 tablespoons) **tequila**, 2 tablespoons cold water, and ice; stir to combine and serve.

MINT JULEP
makes 1

Stir together 1 teaspoon **sugar** and 1 teaspoon water in a glass (or julep cup) until sugar dissolves. Add 8 fresh **mint** leaves, and mash using a muddler or a wooden spoon. Fill with crushed ice, and add 2⅔ ounces (⅓ cup) **bourbon**. Stir until outside of cup is frosted. Garnish with mint sprigs and serve.

MARGARITAS
makes 8

Pour **coarse salt** onto a saucer. Rub rims of 8 glasses with a **lime** wedge; dip each rim in salt. Fill glasses with ice. In a pitcher, combine ¾ cup fresh **lime juice** (from 6 to 8 limes), 6 ounces (¾ cup) best-quality **tequila**, and 3 ounces (¼ cup plus 2 tablespoons) **Triple Sec** or other citrus-flavored liqueur. Strain into glasses. Garnish with lime wedges; serve.

Highballs

VODKA AND PEAR-NECTAR COCKTAILS
makes 6

Fill glasses halfway with ice. Pour ½ ounce (1 tablespoon) **vodka,** ½ cup **pear nectar,** and 1½ ounces (3 tablespoons) **dry white wine** or sparkling wine into each. Stir, garnish with a **rosemary** sprig and a **pear** slice, and serve.

PIMM'S CUPS
makes 10

In a pitcher, combine 1 cup hulled, quartered **strawberries** and 1 each thinly sliced **lemon, lime,** and **orange.** Add 24 ounces (3 cups) **Pimm's No. 1;** mash lightly with a muddler or wooden spoon. Chill up to 4 hours. To serve, fill glasses halfway with ice; add ⅓ cup Pimm's mixture to each. Top with **ginger ale;** stir. Garnish with **cucumber** slices and berries.

NEGRONI SWIZZLE
makes 1

Fill glass with crushed ice. Pour in 1½ ounces (3 tablespoons) each **gin** and **Campari** and ½ ounce (1 tablespoon) **sweet vermouth.** Using tongs, hold 1 strip **orange** peel over a gas burner (or small kitchen torch) until edges are blackened, 5 to 10 seconds. Garnish drink with peel. Top with seltzer, if desired; stir until glass is frosty. Serve immediately.

PISCO SPRITZES
makes 6

Heat ½ cup each sugar and water in a saucepan over high, stirring until sugar dissolves. Let simple syrup cool. Mix 1 cup plus 2 tablespoons chilled **pineapple juice,** 6 ounces (¾ cup) chilled **pisco,** 1 tablespoon simple syrup, and 6 dashes **Angostura bitters** in a pitcher. Divide among glasses; top with 1 bottle (750 mL) **dry sparkling wine.** Serve immediately.

CHICAGO FIZZ
makes 1

Combine 2 ounces (¼ cup) **dark rum**, 2 ounces (¼ cup) **ruby port**, 1 teaspoon **superfine sugar**, 2 tablespoons fresh **lemon** juice, and 1 large **egg** white in a cocktail shaker. Shake briefly, then add ice to fill shaker and shake vigorously for 8 seconds. Strain into a glass and top with club soda, if desired. Serve immediately.

PIÑA COLADAS
makes 4

Puree 3 cups ice, 2 cups unsweetened **pineapple juice**, 8 ounces (1 cup) **dark rum**, and 6 ounces (¾ cup) **cream of coconut** (such as Coco López) in a blender until frothy. Divide among glasses; garnish each with a **pineapple** round, and serve.

SUMMER BLOODY MARY
makes 1

Fill glass with ice cubes, then fill one-third full with **vodka** (preferably tomato-flavored). Squeeze a few **cherry tomatoes** over the ice, then drop them in. Top with **seltzer**. If desired, garnish with a basil sprig and sprinkle with freshly ground pepper.

LILLET-BASIL COCKTAIL
makes 1

Put 1 cup ice, 4 ounces (½ cup) **Lillet Blanc**, 1 ounce (2 tablespoons) **gin**, 2 tablespoons fresh **orange juice**, and ¼ cup **fresh basil** leaves in a cocktail shaker; shake well. Fill a glass with ice; strain mixture into glass. Add a splash of **tonic water**. Garnish with 1 **cucumber** spear, 1 **cinnamon stick**, and a basil sprig. Serve immediately.

Stemmed

MEYER LEMON DROP
makes 1

Heat ½ cup each **sugar** and water with 6 strips **Meyer lemon** zest in a saucepan, stirring, until sugar dissolves. Let syrup cool. In an ice-filled cocktail shaker, combine 2 ounces (¼ cup) vodka, ½ ounce (1 tablespoon) **Cointreau**, 2 tablespoons Meyer lemon juice, and 1 tablespoon lemon syrup; shake well. Strain into a glass. Garnish with a lemon wedge; serve.

MANHATTAN
makes 1

Combine 2 ounces (¼ cup) **rye whiskey** or **bourbon**, 1 ounce (2 tablespoons) **sweet red vermouth**, 2 dashes Angostura **bitters**, and 1 cup ice in a cocktail shaker; shake well. Strain into a chilled glass. Garnish with a **maraschino cherry** and serve.

POM SUNRISE
makes 1

Fill a cocktail shaker with ice. Add ¼ cup fresh **tangerine** juice, 1 ounce (2 tablespoons) **vodka**, and 2 dashes Angostura **bitters.** Shake vigorously; strain into a glass. Discard ice from shaker. Combine 2 tablespoons unsweetened **pomegranate juice** and 1 teaspoon **sugar** in shaker; shake until sugar dissolves. Slowly pour pomegranate mixture into glass and serve.

DIRTY MARTINI
makes 1

In an ice-filled cocktail shaker, shake or stir 4 ounces (½ cup) **vodka** (or gin) and a dash of **olive brine**. Strain into a chilled glass. Garnish with a pimiento olive and serve.

CELERY FRENCH 75
makes 12

Heat ½ cup each **sugar** and water in a sauce-pan over high, stirring until sugar dissolves. Remove from heat; add 2 tablespoons **celery leaves.** Let simple syrup cool. Strain out leaves. Combine 1 table-spoon each syrup and fresh **lemon** juice and ½ ounce (1 tablespoon) **gin** in each glass. Top with 1 bottle (750 mL) **dry sparkling wine;** stir. Garnish with a celery leaf; serve.

RYE DERBY
makes 1

Fill a cocktail shaker with ice. Add 1½ ounces (3 table-spoons) **bourbon** or **rye whiskey,** ½ ounce (1 tablespoon) each **sweet vermouth** and **Grand Marnier,** and 1 tablespoon fresh **lime** juice. Shake well; strain into a chilled glass. Garnish with a thin lime slice and serve.

PLUM BLOSSOM
makes 1

Fill glass with ice. Pour in 2 ounces (¼ cup) **plum wine,** 2 ounces (¼ cup) **dry sake,** and ½ ounce (1 tablespoon) **St-Germain elder-flower liqueur.** Stir to combine. Garnish with 1 **umeboshi plum** (available at Asian markets and international aisle of supermarkets) and serve.

CRANBERRY SPARKLERS
makes 10

In a blender, combine 2 cups fresh or thawed frozen **cranberries,** 1 cup **sugar,** and 1 cup **vodka.** Puree until smooth; then strain and chill. Fill flutes one quarter with cranberry mixture. Tilt flutes and gently pour **sparkling wine** down sides of glasses to create sparkler effect. Serve immediately.

Pitchers and Punches

ORANGE WHEAT SHANDIES
serves 4 to 6

Combine 48 ounces (4 bottles) **wheat beer**, 1 cup fresh **orange** juice, and ¼ teaspoon pure **almond extract** (optional) in a pitcher. Stir well. Serve with thinly sliced orange for garnishes.

SOUR CHERRY MOJITOS
serves 14 to 16

Heat 1¼ cups **sugar** and 1¼ cups water in a saucepan over high, stirring occasionally, until sugar dissolves. Let simple syrup cool. Combine ⅔ cup fresh **lemon** juice, 3 pounds frozen pitted **sour cherries** (partially thawed with juices), and 1 cup **fresh basil** leaves in a bowl. Add syrup; mash lightly to release juices. Refrigerate 1 to 4 days. Combine fruit mixture and 16 to 24 ounces (2 to 3 cups) **vodka** in a pitcher; ladle ⅓ cup into each ice-filled glass. Fill with ice. Top with **sparkling water**, garnish with more basil; serve.

APPLE-CIDER SANGRIA
serves 12 to 14

Freeze 3 cups **green seedless grapes** on a parchment-lined baking sheet. Combine another 3 cups green grapes in a pitcher with 4 peeled and sliced **kiwis** and 8 thinly sliced (seeds removed) small **apples,** such as lady apples. Stir in 1 bottle (750 mL) dry **white wine,** 1 quart pure unfiltered **apple cider,** and 8 ounces (1 cup) **apple brandy,** such as calvados. Cover and refrigerate 4 to 24 hours. Serve in glasses filled partially with frozen grapes.

ARNOLD PALMERS WITH BOURBON
serves 6 to 8

Heat ½ cup **sugar** and ½ cup water in a saucepan over high, stirring occasionally, until sugar dissolves. Let simple syrup cool. Pour 2 cups boiling water over 4 teaspoons loose **English breakfast tea** (or 4 tea bags); cover and steep 5 to 7 minutes. Strain into a pitcher; chill 1 hour and up to 1 day. Stir in 4 ounces (½ cup) **bourbon**, juice of 1 **orange**, juice of 1 **lemon,** and 2 tablespoons simple syrup. Serve over ice with a lemon or orange slice for garnish.

MULLED BLOOD-ORANGE PUNCH
serves 10 to 12

Bring 2 cups fresh **blood-orange** juice, 8 **allspice berries,** 2 **cinnamon** sticks, 1 **star-anise** pod, and 5 cloves to a boil over medium-high heat. Let cool; chill 12 to 24 hours. Strain into a punch bowl; discard spices. Stir in another 2 cups blood-orange juice and 2 cups **orange juice**. Garnish with 1 thinly sliced blood orange. Serve as is or topped with chilled sparkling wine, vodka, or sparkling water.

PINEAPPLE-MINT DAIQUIRIS
serves 10 to 12

Bring 2 chopped peeled **pineapples**, 2 cups water, and ⅓ cup **sugar** to a boil in a pot. Cover; simmer until fruit is tender, 5 minutes. Let cool, then puree, in batches, in a blender. Strain into a bowl; let cool 1 hour. In a pitcher, crush 1 cup chopped fresh **mint** leaves with a muddle or wooden spoon. Stir in pineapple juice; chill 8 to 24 hours. Add 16 ounces (2 cups) **white rum** and ½ cup fresh **lemon juice**. Serve in ice-filled glasses; garnish with more mint leaves.

Basic Recipes and Techniques

TOASTING NUTS AND SEEDS

· To toast nuts such as almonds, walnuts, or pecans: Spread them on a rimmed baking sheet, and cook in a 350°F oven until fragrant, tossing once or twice, about 10 minutes. (Start checking after 6 minutes if toasting sliced or chopped nuts.)

· Toast hazelnuts in a 375°F oven until skins split, 10 to 12 minutes; rub warm nuts in a clean kitchen towel to remove skins.

· Toast pine nuts or pepitas in a small skillet over medium heat, shaking the pan occasionally, until lightly browned, 3 to 5 minutes.

· Toast sesame seeds in a small skillet over medium heat, shaking the pan occasionally, until golden, 2 to 3 minutes (be careful not to let them burn). Transfer to a plate to cool.

MAKING BREADCRUMBS

Trim off crusts from a loaf of bread (Pullman, pandemie, or other type), and tear the bread into large pieces. Pulse in a food processor to form coarse or fine crumbs, as desired. (For dried breadcrumbs, toast in a 250°F oven 12 to 15 minutes.) Breadcrumbs can be frozen, in an airtight container, for up to 3 months.

WASHING LEEKS

Trim and discard root ends and dark-green parts from leeks. Cut leeks into pieces of desired size, then place in a bowl; wash leeks in several changes of cold water, swishing to loosen grit, until you no longer see any grit in bowl. Lift leeks out of water, and dry on a clean kitchen towel (or paper towels).

ROASTING PEPPERS AND CHILES

Roast bell peppers or chiles (such as poblanos) over a gas flame, turning with tongs, until charred all over. (Alternately, char under the broiler, turning as needed.) Transfer to a bowl, cover with a large plate, and let cool. Rub off skins with paper towels, using a knife to remove any stubborn spots. Remove and discard stems, ribs, and seeds.

PEELING AND PITTING MANGO

Remove the peel with a vegetable peeler or sharp knife, following the curve of the fruit. Stand peeled mango upright, and cut along both sides of the large, narrow pit in the center, separating the flesh from it. Cut mango as directed in a recipe.

BLANCHING AND PEELING TOMATOES

Cut a small "X" in the bottom of each tomato. Blanch in a pot of boiling water until skins loosen, about 15 seconds; then use a slotted spoon to transfer to an ice-water bath and let cool completely. Peel off skins and discard.

PEELING AND DEVEINING SHRIMP

Holding shrimp by the tail, peel shell from inside curve with your fingers, leaving tail intact (or remove, if desired). Gently run a paring knife from head to tail, along the center of the back, to expose the "vein." Then use the knife to remove it in one piece.

BASIC PIZZA DOUGH
Makes enough for two 6-by-16-inch pizzas

—

- 1 envelope (2¼ teaspoons) active dry yeast
- 1¼ cups warm water (110°F)
- 1½ teaspoon coarse salt
- 1 teaspoon sugar
- 2 tablespoons extra-virgin olive oil, plus more for bowl
- 3½ cups all-purpose flour, plus more for dusting

1. Sprinkle yeast over the warm water in a large bowl. Let stand until foamy, about 5 minutes. Whisk in salt, sugar, and oil to combine. Stir in flour until a sticky dough forms.

2. Turn out dough onto a lightly floured work surface; knead with floured hands, adding more flour if dough is sticky, until a smooth ball forms, about 1 minute. Place dough in a large oiled bowl, turning dough to evenly coat. Cover with oiled plastic wrap; let rise in a warm, draft-free spot until doubled in bulk, 30 to 40 minutes.

3. Punch down dough. Fold dough back onto itself four or five times, then form into a ball again. Replace plastic wrap; let dough rise again until doubled in bulk, 30 to 40 minutes.

4. Punch down dough; turn out onto a lightly floured surface. Divide dough in half. Use immediately or refrigerate, wrapped well in plastic, up to 1 day; bring to room temperature before using.

NUOC CHAM DIPPING SAUCE
makes 1½ cups

- ¼ cup plus 2 tablespoons fresh lime juice (from about 6 limes)
- ¼ cup plus 2 tablespoons fish sauce, such as nam pla
- ¼ cup plus 2 tablespoons unseasoned rice vinegar
- 2½ teaspoons sugar
- 1 to 2 fresh chiles, such as Thai bird, very thinly sliced (seeds and ribs removed if less heat is desired)

Stir together ingredients in a bowl until sugar has dissolved. Sauce can be refrigerated, covered, up to 3 hours; bring to room temperature before serving.

PEANUT DIPPING SAUCE
makes 1¼ cups

- 1 teaspoon safflower oil
- 2 garlic cloves, minced
- 2 tablespoons tomato paste
- 2 tablespoons hoisin sauce
- ½ cup creamy peanut butter

  Roasted unsalted peanuts, coarsely chopped, for garnish

1. Heat oil in a small saucepan over medium-high. Add garlic, tomato paste, and hoisin; cook, stirring, until mixture comes to a boil, about 1 minute. Add ¼ cup peanut butter and 1 cup water; return to a boil, whisking until mixture is smooth and combined.

2. Reduce heat to medium-low and simmer until thickened and slightly darkened, 3 minutes. Remove from heat; whisk in remaining ¼ cup peanut butter and ¼ cup water, and let cool. Dipping sauce can be refrigerated, covered, up to 3 days; bring to room temperature and garnish with peanuts before serving.

ROMESCO SAUCE
Makes about 1½ cups

- ¼ cup blanched almonds, toasted (see page 242)
- 1 garlic clove
- 1 jar (10 ounces) roasted piquillo peppers, drained
- ¼ cup extra-virgin olive oil
- 2 teaspoons sherry vinegar

Pulse almonds and garlic in a food processor until coarsely ground. Add peppers, oil, and vinegar, and puree until smooth. Sauce can be refrigerated, covered, up to 1 day before serving.

Acknowledgments
—

If there's one thing shared by all of us at Martha Stewart Living, it's an enthusiasm for hosting friends and families. The talented and dedicated team behind this new book (our 85th!) is especially devoted to the subject, as you can tell by the book you hold in your hands. A big thank-you to: executive editor Evelyn Battaglia; food editor Greg Lofts; editorial director Ellen Morrissey; managing editor Susanne Ruppert; design director Jennifer Wagner; deputy art director Gillian MacLeod; design production associate John Myers; and editorial assistant Christopher Rudolph. Thanks as well to chief content director Eric A. Pike for his guidance, and to the rest of the MSL food team, led by Lucinda Scala Quinn and Jennifer Aaronson, for the foolproof recipes that make up this collection.

We very much appreciate all the others at MSL who contributed to the book, including Shira Bocar, Sarah Carey, Denise Clappi, Linda Denahan, Allison Vanek Devine, Spyridon Ginis, Tanya Graf, Katie Holdefehr, Eleanor McQuistion, Ryan Monaghan, Ayesha Patel, Laura Rege, and Sarah Vasil.

Thanks also to Nicole Coppola, Camila de Onis, Tessa Liebman, Nanette Maxim, Katherine McElhiney, Michele Outland, and Lauren Tyrell for their assistance.

We are especially grateful to talented photographer David Malosh, who provided all but a couple of the mouth-watering images, aided by Ashley Corbin-Teich.

As always, we are so pleased and delighted to collaborate with our longtime partners at Clarkson Potter and Crown, especially publisher Aaron Wehner, associate publisher Doris Cooper, editor Ashley Phillips, art directors Stephanie Huntwork and Michael Nagin, production director Linnea Knollmueller, and senior production editor Patricia Shaw. Thanks also to Sean Boyles, Carly Gorga, Maya Mavjee, and Kate Tyler.

And we are ever grateful to our loyal readers and customers, who inspire us to do everything we do.

Index

—

About the Author

—

Martha Stewart, founder of Martha Stewart Living Omnimedia, is America's most trusted lifestyle expert and teacher. Her first book, *Entertaining*, was published in 1982, and since then she has authored dozens of bestselling books on cooking, gardening, weddings, homekeeping, and decorating, including *Martha Stewart's Baking Handbook, Martha Stewart's Encyclopedia of Crafts, Martha Stewart's Cooking School, Martha's American Food, One Pot, Clean Slate*, and many more.

MSLO publishes two award-winning magazines, *Martha Stewart Living* and *Martha Stewart Weddings;* designs branded merchandise for a broad group of retailers; and provides a wealth of inspired ideas and practical information at marthastewart.com.

Copyright © 2015 by
Martha Stewart Living
Omnimedia, Inc.

All rights reserved. Published
in the United States by
Clarkson Potter/Publishers,
an imprint of the Crown
Publishing Group, a division
of Penguin Random House LLC,
New York.

www.crownpublishing.com
www.clarksonpotter.com

CLARKSON POTTER is
a trademark and POTTER
with colophon is a
registered trademark of
Penguin Random House LLC.

Selected photographs and
recipes appeared in previous
Martha Stewart Living
publications.

Library of Congress
Cataloging-in-Publication Data

Martha Stewart's appetizers /
editors of Martha Stewart Living.
— First edition.
    pages cm
  Includes index.
1. Appetizers. I. Stewart,
Martha. II. Martha Stewart
Living Omnimedia. III. Martha
Stewart Living. IV. Title:
Appetizers.
TX740.M283 2015
641.81'2—dc23

ISBN 978-0-307-95462-6
eBook ISBN 978-0-307-95463-3

Printed in China

Book design by
Gillian MacLeod

Cover photographs by
David Malosh

All photographs by
David Malosh, except
the following: Marcus
Nilsson (page 185),
Burcu Avsar (page 226),
and Fadil Berisha (page 255)

10 9 8 7 6 5 4 3 2 1

First Edition